ENDORSEMENTS

Bigger Things by Vineyard pastor and leader Melt van der Spuy is a terrific and rollicking read. Absolutely crammed with robust theology, practical orthopraxy and personal anecdotes, it is a helpful guide for Christian leaders and pastors trying to navigate the way forward with hurricane force winds coming from all directions.

Larry Levy, Halifax Metro Vineyard Church
and USA/Canada Vineyard Partnership
Coordinator for East Africa

Just when I'd shrunk my kingdom expectations down to something tame, manageable and small, Melt's book dropped into my hands and provoked me to consider *Bigger Things*. Not flaky, trendy or provincial things—but things that matter, things that are durable, things that deserve my re-kindled attention. I wasn't expecting this: solid theology wrapped in a riveting story and prayed over me by a guy with a huge heart. Thank you Melt.

Brady Wilson, thought leader, author,
keynote speaker and co-founder of Juice Inc.

Simple yet profound. Simple because the author's theology is embedded in the author's story. Profound in that that same theology is thought-provoking, challenging, and rich. Written predominantly to and for the Vineyard movement, *Bigger Things* deserves a wider audience. Especially for those in any form of leadership. I look forward to reading it again.

Michael Arnold, Anglican priest,
school chaplain, and author of *The Forgotten Feast*

"From the overflow of the heart the mouth speaks." To read *Bigger Things* is to be drawn into the reflective, authentic and conversational flow of Melt's long obedience in the same direction. Weaving between narrative memoir, political commentary, deep theology, and a hint of sass, Melt reaches into his depth of lived experience, and pastorally calls the Vineyard back to an integrated, holistic radical middle. *Bigger Things* is refreshing in its cadence, inviting us to steep in the deep truths of Scripture and orthodoxy, while also being curiously and expectantly awake to the work of the Spirit. A worthy read!

Krista Heide, artist, spiritual director,
pastoral ministry leader in Vineyard Canada

Like an archer drawing the string back, Melt van der Spuy takes aim at tensions within the charismatic movement. With humility, theological depth, and clarity, he releases a word that flies true. *Bigger Things* doesn't shy away from the messiness of renewal, nor does it settle for nostalgic retellings. Instead, Melt invites us into a courageous reframing—holding critique and hope in dynamic tension, tethered to the ancient path and animated by the Spirit's living work. This book lands its arrow true—calling the Church back to her missional core, away from shallow triumphalism, and toward a Spirit-empowered, Christ-centered renewal. With the wisdom of an elder and the heart of a shepherd, Melt helps us reimagine what renewal might look like.

Todd Rutkowski, author, storyteller,
culture shaper, Vineyard pastor and leader

Melt van der Spuy offers timely course correction and an excellent primer in the priorities of the Kingdom of God. It is timely, because the church today is continually beset by worldly values that skew theological thinking. The idea of "dominionism," where "power over" has eclipsed Jesus' Kingdom teaching of "powerless power" and loving others, is one example of how Melt refreshes our Kingdom memory. *Bigger Things* directs the reader to the sometimes unseen or ignored arc of God's purpose. Melt points to responsible hermeneutics as key to unraveling pop theology and debunking bandwagon trends in the church today, trends which few are willing to challenge for fear of not toeing the party line.

Bigger Things is not about big events or "bigger is better." It is about how we are to live and grow in the character of Jesus, resisting the world's ways. It is about how to use the gifts or tools the Holy Spirit has given us responsibly. It is about how the Father plays out His "long game" of redemption through us when we listen and submit to the bigger things God is doing.

Rev. Rik Berry, Ph.D., Vineyard pastor and regional team leader for Vineyard National Team in Canada

BIGGER THINGS

REFRAMING RENEWAL
THROUGH THE LENS OF
HISTORICALLY BIBLICAL ORTHODOXY

MELT W. VAN DER SPUY

FOREWORD BY DAVID RUIS

BIGGER THINGS

REFRAMING RENEWAL THROUGH THE LENS OF HISTORICALLY BIBLICAL ORTHODOXY

WIPF & STOCK · Eugene, Oregon

BIGGER THINGS

Reframing Renewal Through the Lens of Historically Biblical Orthodoxy

Wipf & Stock
An Imprint of Wipf and Stock Publishers
199 W. 8th Ave., Suite 3
Eugene, OR 97401

www.wipfandstock.com

PAPERBACK ISBN: 979-8-3852-7041-5
HARDCOVER ISBN: 979-8-3852-7042-2
EBOOK ISBN: 979-8-3852-7043-9

To contact the author: melt.vanderspuy@newjoychurch.com

Cover Design by Simone Rowe

Book Layout and Publishing Support by
PearCreative.ca

Edited by Lauren Balfour

To my wife Anida, and our kids who
have come along for the ride and stayed the course.

CONTENTS

FOREWORD

"It's so easy to separate the teaching from the teacher and live as though we don't really need Christ, we just need the teachings. Everything is actually embedded in the person and the story of Christ. His story needs to become our story."

STANLEY HAUERWAS

Theology matters. Full stop. That's why I'm so glad my friend and colleague has written this book for our consideration.

But to surmise that this is purely an academic exercise, or a discipline required to ensure that one is "right" in these matters, is to miss the *heart* of the matter. Entirely.

And Melt gets that.

So, *Bigger Things* is really a book about reaching for what matters.

As I attempt to introduce you to Melt and his work, one persistent observation comes to mind. He is a bit of a romantic in the classic sense of the term. I don't know if I've ever quite met anyone who loves—feels—as deeply as Melt. He loves people—I mean *loves* people. He loves life. Whether it's swinging a golf club with a few mates, cheering for his beloved Springboks or soaking up a sunset cascading over a rolling vineyard scape, his passion is contagious. He loves to laugh. Have you ever heard him laugh? You must one day if you haven't yet. He loves to study. He loves to question and tussle with meaning. He loves to preach. And yes, he loves theology. So this book, while satisfyingly intellectual, comes from the heart.

While exhibiting pretty much all the characteristics of romanticism—in essence celebrating the power of emotion, imagination, intuition, and story as much as that of reason and logic—Melt is unwavering in his commitment to the belief that there *is* a truth that transcends, and indeed anchors, us to something objective. Something holy. Or may I say, someOne. And wouldn't you know it, that One—our God—is succinctly, mysteriously, and powerfully spoken of in 1 John 4:8 like this: "God is love."

As a theologian then, for Melt has earned a doctorate from Fuller Theological Seminary, his intellectual pursuits have always compelled him to move towards people and away from some ivory tower. For love compels. Love calls. Love cannot be stagnant and remain love. This has taken him into pastoral ministry in the local church where he remains to this day, as well as significant leadership with various NPOs and involvement in consulting and conflict resolution in both the church world and in commerce.

A romantic. A theologian. But let me introduce one other facet of who I know Melt to be, which forcefully comes through in his writing: a practitioner. Trained in systematics, but a narrative theologian in the way he communicates. He is African after all! When I think of Paul's lament in 1 Corinthians 4:15, that though we have "countless guides in Christ—ten thousand instructors," we have few fathers, I think, well at least we have Melt!

And so here we find him, in this book of his, full circle. His theological quest, the study of God, has been not just knowing about God or even experiencing God, but allowing his life to be transformed day by day into the image and likeness of this God become flesh, Jesus, and in that constant surrendering, discovering the marvelous and beautiful empowering filling of the Holy Spirit. And yes, a calling. A calling to serve the Church, and not only serve, but to be a part. To embrace community in all its mess and beauty, joy and frustration, suffering, and glory.

So really, when you boil it all down, *love matters most.* And Melt gets that.

I invite you to read this book with the eyes and heart of the romantic. To listen to the stories of God, the Kingdom, the people, and the man as they created echoes and harmonies that are in sync with a hunger for Truth that bleeds through these pages. To learn, not simply to gain knowledge or understanding, but to learn. To become. To reach for the "Bigger Things."

DAVID RUIS

National Director, Association of Vineyard Churches, Canada

ACKNOWLEDGEMENTS

There are many people I need to thank for this book. In one sense, all the characters and the churches and the organisations that feature need to be thanked. All those people and spaces have shaped me, mostly for good, into who I am and equipped me to offer whatever it is I might have to offer. So, thank you all! And thank you to the God and father of Jesus, who has brought me to those people, spaces, and places. Life in the Kingdom is a journey indeed.

But more to the point of the book itself. Firstly, Anida, my wife, who has been way more supportive over the ups and downs of the years than I have ever fully and publicly given her credit for. Thank you for staying the course. I love you. Our kids and sons-in-law, who (to their likely dismay) feature somewhat in the book, are all amazing. I could not wish for a better family.

This book began when Todd Rutkowski asked me to review his book *Our Beautiful Mess* as a content reader, checking theology throughout—any heresy in his book is down to me. It was the second book I had been asked to review theologically, the first one being Michael Arnold's *The Forgotten Feast.*

In the process, I felt the Spirit prompting me that I might have something to say myself and needed to start writing. And so, I started writing *Bigger Things* in January of 2025. Thank you Todd for the kick start I needed, and for so much more.

Thank you to David Ruis, who although not (at short notice) the co-author I had initially hoped for, has contributed a beautiful foreword as well as much toward the section on the prophetic. We will certainly collaborate more in the future. David's insight is profound, and I have drawn significantly from it. Having said that, all views in the book are mine alone.

Thank you to Krista Heide, who is meant to be a mentee of mine at an academic level, but is something of a mentor to me too. In the early stages of the book Krista clarified a few key concepts and is one of the most profound strategic thinkers I have met.

Thank you to Daile Unruh-Peters for her content reading and egalitarian sensitivities that helped this crusty old white guy make sure I was using language consistent with my stated positions.

Thank you to Lauren Balfour for the meticulous editing. I tend to write from the heart and overstate. I worry about the truth first and then go back and try to make it better later. Lauren has been most helpful in toning things down where needed without ripping the heart out of it. Lauren edited my doctoral project for Fuller in 2021, and I hope that we can collaborate again. You are easy to work with—thank you.

To my daughter Simone Rowe, who is ridiculously gifted. Thank you for the cover design, the creative ideas and for living with the old man's quirks. Your communication skills still need some work, but for the rest you are just brilliant!

Thank you to Yvonne Parks, who came in late and helped the project toward its conclusion. Yvonne, your openness to collaborate with the work that was already done, your willingness to allow for my own preferences, and your professional experience in navigating everything entailed in bringing a book to fruition and to market are appreciated and will no doubt be called upon again.

Thank you, David Clemens, for checking my rudimentary Greek. Your presence in worship makes me more careful about things of which I only know the basics. Thank you to all who have read and provided endorsements. I appreciate you all.

Thank you to my "Cansaffrican" compatriot Willie Jacobs for reading along and our conversations following from his reading. *Jy is n baie slim man, maar ook n' baie opregte man Willie. Dit is goed om jou n' vriend te noem.*

Lastly, thanks to a group of friends in Calgary who may be surprised that they feature at all. We are mostly, but not always, connected via a chat group. Todd Rutkowski, Art Rae and Daniel Schuster. Thank you for your hospitality. Thank you for reminding me and keeping me true to what God has called me to here in Canada. Thank you for welcoming Anida and me into the fold, even seeking me out when I've been doing various rounds across the country. There was a night when you all drove 104 kilometers from Calgary to Canmore to have dinner with me because you knew I was travelling alone. Only real friends would do that. Thank you. There have, as you know, been times when I've been tempted to chuck it in and head back to African skies. Your sincere, authentic and non-judgmental friendship and ability to hold one another accountable, often in jest, has been a necessary lifeline to me.

Langley, BC
April 2025

PREFACE

"Love without courage and wisdom is sentimentality, as with the ordinary church member. Courage without love and wisdom is foolhardiness, as with the ordinary soldier. Wisdom without love and courage is cowardice, as with the ordinary intellectual. But the one who has love, courage, and wisdom moves the world."

AMMON HENNACY

For some years I have been toying with the idea of a first book. My writing endeavors have been limited to academic writing, sermon writing, and to a lesser extent some reflective and devotional writing when called upon to do that. My inclination is unapologetically theological. My goal in that is always to take theology out of the academy and to make it more accessible and useful to every follower of Jesus. Having had both feet in the local church, with forays into sessional teaching and academic writing over the last twenty-five years, positions me well for such a task. I had started to outline something on the confusion between God's kingdom and earthly empires in 2021 after completing a doctorate at Fuller Seminary. Thankfully, my hard drive crashed, and I had not backed up my provisional ramblings. I say thankfully, because having read most of the works of Yoder and Hauerwas, and more recently Tom

Wright, Mike Bird,[1] and Philip Jenkins, on earthly empires and Jesus in the political or public sphere, I realize now that I would not have added anything significant to what has already been offered.

> The sometime alliance of Church and empire has plagued the Church at various times in history since her inception.

From a love of the Vineyard churches and the broader charismatic movement, I have settled on a more modest but also more directional and intentional quest. *Bigger Things* aims to speak directly to the stream I call spiritual home: the Vineyard churches. I hope too that the book will gain a broader readership within the greater world of charismatic churches.

Certainly, I hope to at least speak to those charismatics who are not overtly anti-intellectual or anti-theological. To be honest, I have always wondered at the practice of separating out the work of the Holy Spirit neatly into signs and wonders and the charismata. Scriptures such as 2 Timothy 2:15 and Romans 12:2 speak clearly of our minds. The charismatic churches collectively might need more than just a small correction. Any correction will need to come from within the charismatic churches themselves if it is to be received at any level. As a colleague and friend David Ross says in his PhD thesis: "It is time for the renewal of the renewal movement."

When I came to faith in 1990, the biggest elephant in the evangelical room seemed to me to be the divide between the ***cessationist*** and dispensational camp on one hand versus the Pentecostal and neo-Charismatic churches on the other.

Cessationism teaches that the miraculous gifts of the Holy Spirit ceased around the time of the end of the apostolic era when the last of the apostles died.

In no small way, the Vineyard movement had stood, along with many others of like mind, as a via-media between the **under- and over-realised eschatologies** that were, and to a real extent still are, clear among the followers of Jesus. Vineyards' theology has at its base an **inaugurated eschatology**,[2] which includes a theology of the cross and recognizes the New Testament sign of suffering. Historically, Vineyard mostly avoided triumphal extremism, which set it apart from most other neo-Charismatics of the time.

Under-realised eschatology sees the coming of Kingdom only as a future event. An **over-realised eschatology** essentially sees the Kingdom as already come in all its fullness. **Inaugurated eschatology** recognizes that we live life between the coming of the Kingdom in Jesus and his future consummation of that Kingdom. These different understandings and emphases all have profound implications for life and ministry.

With a growing body of current literature that pleas for a balanced eschatology, there is an increased understanding across denominations of what it means for us practically to live between the ages.

I want to draw attention to the New Testament teaching that suffering for the sake of Jesus is *the* one consistently observable sign on those who are called to follow Jesus. It is in every way a sign *and a gift* that is promised more than any other sign in the New Testament. This is not to glorify some kind of deluded martyrdom complex, but to recognise that the charismatic movement in general has ignored the prolific sign of suffering that is there in the NT and has erred toward prosperity ("health and wealth") teaching that has little if any New Testament undergirding.[3]

Living between the ages means that any inbreaking of the kingdom we receive is only a foreshadow (Col 2:17). However energizing and life-giving it is for us, any building we do for the kingdom now[4] is at best, partial. It somehow mysteriously accompanies us into the new kingdom (Rev 21:24), but it is not a finished product, or we would not be praying "Lord, let it be on earth, as it already is in the heavenlies."

When I came to faith in Jesus thirty-five years ago, I found myself in a local church where I was told that I was apparently not supposed to be having some of the experiences I was having. That meant I was not allowed to share that I was called to follow Jesus through an open vision in the middle of Cape Town in which all the people and buildings had disappeared and only Table Mountain was before me and the Atlantic Ocean behind me. I was made to deny some of what God had done and was doing in me, despite that being my honest conversion story. In time, the fact that I could not appropriately share these things without being looked at as if I needed to be institutionalised led me into more charismatic circles. Initially I moved into, and was ordained into, the New Wine Anglican renewalist churches in the Anglican Diocese of Cape Town.[5] In 2006, I settled with the inner-city Vineyard church we had been partnering with.[6] I had come to recognize that as hard as I tried to be a good Anglican, as my wife Anida reminded me, I really was more fully at home with a group of erstwhile hippies and vagabonds.

Whilst the extreme of cessationism still exists, the explosive growth of the Pentecostal and charismatic churches throughout the world has been unparalleled. The charismatics have won the battle, so to speak. *At the very least, they have won it numerically.* This groundswell of charismatic growth, as exciting and as incredible as most of it has been, has seen the infiltration of various practices into Church worship that may not always be helpful. It has also seen the omission of advised biblical practices—such as communal weighing of the prophetic—that has, at times, damaged the overall witness of the charismatic movement. What began as a fresh, exciting, encouraging rediscovery, and re-emphasising of the beauty in the ***charismata*** of healing, deliverance, tongues, miracles, and prophecy has—in some locations and contexts—become quite Corinthian (1 Cor 5:1). In spaces like these, there is little sign of the love without which the charismata make no sense and are bankrupt (1 Cor 13:1).

> The ***charismata*** are the graces or gifts that are spoken of in 1 Corinthians and Romans and are most likely examples of the kinds of gifts God gives to believers rather than exhaustive lists of what the gifts may be limited to.

The challenges facing the charismatic movement overlap only somewhat with the challenges addressed in a (now) plethora of books on Jesus in the public sphere. These books warn of the dangers of white Christian Nationalism, triumphalism and dominionism, patriarchy, and a general posture that is at odds with any mandate Jesus gives us in the Sermon on the Mount. Although the challenges are different, by all appearances they seem to stem from similar root causes.

> If the problem lies in the same underlying beliefs and practices, then the solution needs to reside in similar theological corrections. People do not necessarily live what they profess, but they always live what they truly believe.

Some identified root causes are dealt with as chapters in this book. They include, in no particular order: a significantly over-realised eschatology, a lack of leadership accountability, a theological posture vested more in neo-Platonism and Gnosticism than in a discernably New Testament posture, the adoption of human power-based models for Church leadership, and an occasionally disturbing arrogance and lack of integrity. This means that any corrective for us needs to consider some of the same issues that are covered by Wright, Bird, Hauerwas, Willemon, Du Mez, Jenkins, and others. But in this case, these things will be dealt with specifically as they relate to the Vineyard movement, and to a limited extent, the broader charismatic movement. A reaffirmation of Vineyards' theology and a potential theological undergirding for charismatic churches who may not have a solid undergirding theological foundation will be one aim of this book. That will include chapters on the need for interpretation, inaugurated eschatology, and the combination of a theology of the cross and of the coming of the Kingdom.

As strange as this may sound to any reader whose tradition is Reformed or from other historical churches, not a few charismatics live in the experiential without any meaningful undergirding theology that keeps them from losing their anchoring. In those circles, Scripture is sometimes used without any ***hermeneutic*** at all, let alone a rigorous one. In spaces like these the text often gets reduced to an almost magic status, where the very words "carry power" and what is done with those words is done misguidedly, sometimes in the name of the prophetic.[7]

> ***Hermeneutics*** **is the theory and methodology of interpretation of biblical texts.**

For those wanting to anchor themselves in the ancient paths that the Church has trodden over the centuries *without discounting the experiential* as untrustworthy, *Bigger Things* hopes to offer a modest undergirding theology and practices that will keep us open to the experiential without losing orthodoxy in the process. A theology that uses the Scriptures sensibly and responsibly, in a posture of listening and with great care.

In general, without any suggestion that the historical churches have it all right on every score (who does?), it would seem that the charismatic churches emerging from and remaining within the historical churches (Anglican, Methodist, Presbyterian and so on) are *less likely to err toward what we used to call apostasy* than the independent churches. The historical churches tend to retain the creeds, the spiritual disciplines, things like the *Anglican Prayer Book*, and so on, which seem to hold them in orthodoxy better than many independent churches.

This book includes content on reading the Bible backwards through a Christo-centric, or Messianic, lens. This also means reaffirming the ancient creeds read through the lens of the coming of the Kingdom, which was sufficient for the orthodoxy of the Early Church and therefore is sufficient for us. Additionally, there is some discussion on neo-Platonic thought and Gnosticism alongside their ever-present modern-day equivalents that will be considered. Such parameters aim to keep us on the ancient paths without the non-biblical posture of discounting the experiential. The things that the Church collective throughout the ages has affirmed as the essentials of our "rule of faith" and our "rule of life," in a sense that might be regarded as a safety net. Some might consider them as negative protections, although I do not see it that way.

> This book reaffirms the ancient creeds read through the lens of the coming of the Kingdom, which was sufficient for the orthodoxy of the Early Church and therefore is sufficient for us.

Whilst the current reality in the broader charismatic movement necessitates that certain things are considered with caution, it is not my intention for *Bigger Things* to be a scathing critique of a space I call home. I want to have what Walter Thiessen calls a "strong back-bone and a soft bosom."[8] The call is ultimately to *reframe and reimagine.*

> Or, as Richard Foster recently said, to "work together and walk together, always aiming to stride cheerfully across the earth, serving with as little fanfare as possible."[9] In this, "May God give you the gift of tears. As you walk on this tired and sad earth, may you have the gift of weeping, of a soft heart."

As a Vineyard leader who is now in his early sixties, my desire is to come as an elder rather than with a big stick. I have made peace with the fact that I have morphed from being a "son of thunder" to being a resident elder. The thrust of the book *will be intentionally positive.* It will focus on the possibility for a reframed charismatic theology, and a reimagination of what we have missed in times of renewal. In our excitement at what God has done and is doing among us, we have often missed the bigger things. It is expanded thought on these bigger and missional things that will form the second and main goal of the book. The "what has God been doing and saying to us in general?" and "where have we gone wrong or how can we do this better?" part of the book. It would seem that when the Spirit is moving in the way that the Spirit moves during times of renewal, we get caught up in things that are meant to be realigning us back to Jesus and to his mission of partnering in and planting for the Kingdom. Human tendency is to become so animated at the things that are not really the thing. The things that only ever point to our king. It is these bigger missional things that will be considered as a call to *renewing our missional centre.*

To close the preface, I highlight just one biblical narrative and show how historically we might have missed the main point of the narrative because of a fixation on the things that are not the thing. In Acts 2:4-12 (ESV), at the coming of the Holy Spirit, Luke tells us:

> *And they were all filled with the Holy Spirit and began to speak in other tongues as the Spirit gave them utterance. Now there were dwelling in Jerusalem Jews, devout men from every nation under heaven. And at this sound the multitude came together, and they were bewildered, because each one was hearing them speak in his own language. And they were amazed and astonished, saying, "Are not all these who are speaking Galileans? And how is it that we hear, each of us in his own native language? Parthians and Medes and Elamites and residents of Mesopotamia, Judea and Cappadocia, Pontus*

> *and Asia, Phrygia and Pamphylia, Egypt and the parts of Libya belonging to Cyrene, and visitors from Rome, both Jews and proselytes, Cretans and Arabians—we hear them telling in our own tongues the mighty works of God." And all were amazed and perplexed, saying to one another, "What does this mean?"*

The sign of ***Xenolalia*** or ***Akoulalia*** on display in this first collective New Testament outpouring of the Holy Spirit has received so much attention over centuries in the Church. With the coming of the Pentecostal revivals in Azuza Street at the turn of the twentieth century, the focus was on tongues as *the* sign gift, illustrating God's call into the Kingdom. This was true even for those of us who, like me, believe that tongues is *a* sign gift rather than *the* sign gift. The apostle Paul says tongues is the very least of the gifts.[10]

> ***Xenolalia*** is the ability given to the speaker to speak a foreign language. ***Akoulalia*** is the ability given to the hearer to hear a foreign language in one's own language.

Even for this group, we tend to have missed the bigger thing God was doing. Clearly the bigger thing was missional. It was the uniting of Parthians and Medes and Elamites and residents of Mesopotamia, Judea and Cappadocia, Pontus and Asia, Phrygia and Pamphylia, Egypt and the parts of Libya belonging to Cyrene, and visitors from Rome, both Jews and proselytes, Cretans and Arabians. It was, and still is, the breaking down of ethnic and other barriers that divide and separate people. It was an illustration of the incredible resurrection power of

Jesus that brings whole people groups together. *People who hated one another were united because of Jesus.*

> It was shades of Russia befriending the Ukraine. It was Israel and Palestine reconciled. It was the demise of the demonic ideology of apartheid. It was the Berlin wall coming down. It was recompense to indigenous peoples of the world who have been robbed and oppressed. It was Afro-American men getting a fair rap in the USA. It was women everywhere being recognised and appreciated considering Galatians 3:28, rather than bigoted patriarchs hiding behind selected and poorly interpreted Bible verses.

It was and remains the bigger thing that came about because of the gift of tongues, whether Glosolalia, Akoulalia or Xenolalia. In the power of the resurrected Jesus, God is way bigger than whatever divides us. It was and remains Jesus' self-chosen mandate for his life and ministry, from Isaiah 61:1-3 (NIV):

> *The Spirit of the Sovereign LORD is on me,*
> *because the Lord has anointed me*
> *to proclaim the good news to the poor.*
> *He has sent me to bind up the*
> *brokenhearted,*
> *to proclaim freedom for the captives*
> *and release from darkness for the prisoners*
> *to proclaim the year of the LORD's favour*
> *and the day of vengeance of our God,*
> *to comfort all who mourn,*

and provide for those who grieve in Zion—
to bestow on them a crown of beauty
instead of ashes,
the oil of joy
instead of mourning,
and a garment of praise
instead of a spirit of despair.
They will be called oaks of righteousness,
a planting of the LORD
for the display of his splendour.

> Do all the good you can, by all the means you can, and in all the ways you can, and in all the places you can, and at all the times that you can, and to all the people you can, as long as you ever can.
>
> JOHN WESLEY, 1791

The resurrection of Jesus has the power to unite what has been divided. The Church is a heavenly colony on earth[11] reflecting heavenly unity, rather than earthly division over the use of the gift of tongues! Clearly, this is the bigger thing that Pentecost ushers in. Come Lord Jesus, come Holy Spirit, come and show us more of the same.

CHAPTER 1

THE MIRACLE OF THE EARLY CHURCH

"Diversity is not about how we differ. Diversity is about embracing one another's uniqueness."

OLA JOSEPH

In the preface to *Bigger Things,* I tried to show that in Acts 2 at the coming of the Holy Spirit at Pentecost, the biggest thing might not have been the miracle of tongues. The miracle of tongues was really the means to the bigger thing. The bigger thing was and is that in the resurrection of Jesus and in the coming of the Holy Spirit, Babel was tangibly reversed. The small miracle was tongues. The bigger thing was that people groups of every difference imaginable were united.

The division of human languages into different tongues and dialects at the tower of Babel created a climate that was ripe for disagreement, confusion and conflict amongst the different peoples of the world (Gen 11:1-9). So much conflict and strife in the world now still boils down to worldview and cultural and linguistic differences. Simply put, we really do not go out of our way to better understand and value one another. We tend to place our own cultures and languages on a pedestal. But from the beginning, God intended to unite humanity from all regions, dialects, and ethnicities into a new people, a new creation who would proclaim his glory. In our brokenness humanity reaches the place where we unite against our creator at Babel, and the biblical narrative tells us God confused our languages as a result. We continued to procreate and fill the earth as commanded—that is the one commandment we seem not to have struggled with—but God hindered our ability to unite against him.

> From the beginning, God intended to unite humanity from all regions, dialects, and ethnicities into a new people, a new creation who would proclaim his glory.

Initially, God works within the limitations of his chosen people Israel. Israel was meant to be the lifeboat that rescued humanity, but it fails. God calls one tribe and tongue—the people of Israel—as his witness to the nations (Ex 34:10; Deut 4:1–8, 26:18–19; John 4:19–24). Under the old covenant, the praise of God was limited mostly to this one people. But God wants this one people to make him known to all peoples. "How odd of God/To choose the Jews," wrote William Norman Ewer. Odd or not, this is how God decides to work. And this is how God desires to make himself known to all peoples. But Israel fails miserably. And so, the prophets look to a day when the Lord would unite people from all nations to praise him (Isa 60, Zech 14:16). The outpouring of the Spirit at Pentecost begins this long-anticipated day.

> Pentecost is the festival of the first fruits of the harvest. The Church receives the first fruits of God's cosmic redemption plan when the Holy Spirit is poured out equally upon all humanity (Acts 2:1–4).

The miracle of tongues at Pentecost, where everyone hears the Gospel in his own language, shows how God was breaking down the cultural and ethnic divisions imposed at Babel, revealing that the true Israel is defined not by tongue, ethnicity or culture, but by common faith in Jesus the Messiah (Acts 2:5-11).

When we read the account of Pentecost now, we tend to minimise the miracle of the uniting of peoples as a new creation in Christ. In the ancient world it was not that my neighbour is a little bit racist. Many of the people groups despised one another literally unto death. Sadly, and disturbingly, we are seeing the reemergence of this kind of prejudice in our own time. The cultural diversity of the Early Church *was a countercultural marvel.* Ethnic conflict in the Ancient Near East was severe. Mass violence and genocides were common.

> The region was characterized by military empires that conquered and absorbed the cultures of neighbouring civilizations. State sponsored violence was commonplace. The Assyrians poisoned the wells of their enemies. Romans crucified people. It was a cruel, divided and violent world.

The books of Romans and Hebrews consider how the Jewish Christians, who had been banished from the city of Rome and were now allowed back, were going to need to be able to worship with their Gentile brothers and sisters. Jewish and Gentile believers together at the Church in Rome is in part what the book of Romans is about. Into this cultural melting pot and into this ethnic division and hatred come the followers of Jesus. In Antioch, where Christians are first called Christians, we read:

> *Now those who were scattered because of the persecution that arose over Stephen traveled as far as Phoenicia and Cyprus and Antioch, speaking the word to no one except Jews. But there were some of them, men of Cyprus and Cyrene, who on coming to Antioch spoke to the Hellenists also, preaching the Lord Jesus. And the hand of the Lord was with them, and a great number who believed turned to the Lord. (Acts 11:19-21, ESV)*

From this text alone we see that the Early Church had Libyans, Greeks, Cypriots, Jews, and Phoenicians as part of the congregation. When we add the nationalities referred to in Acts 2, we can add "Parthians and Medes and Elamites and residents of Mesopotamia, Judea and Cappadocia, Pontus and Asia, Phrygia and Pamphylia, Egypt and the parts of Libya belonging to Cyrene, and visitors from Rome, both Jews and proselytes, Cretans and Arabians." Here is a beautiful picture that foreshadows Revelation 7:9 which indicates that every nation, tribe, and tongue will be represented at the banquet of the Lamb.

> If this is what the future looks like and we are doing the works of the Kingdom now, in anticipation of the day when Jesus makes all things new, then this is a picture of what our communities could and should look like now!

Of course, linguistic, gender, ethnic, and cultural differences and tensions all remain with us today, but the power of the Spirit is meant to enable the Church to break through these differences for the sake of the Gospel of the Kingdom. The reversal of Babel has begun, as the ***ecclesia*** from every nation gather before the Lord's throne to worship him (Rev 7:9–12).

> Before the formation of the Church, ***ecclesia*** **(εκκλησια)** simply meant a gathering of people or a general assembly. In time it came to indicate a gathering of citizens to make decisions about the city. It was a central institution in the democracy of ancient Greece. Early Christians adopted the word to refer to the church. Later it specifically came to mean those who had been called by Jesus and set apart for his service.

In modern times the increase in diversity of language and culture seen in most Western countries, coupled with ethnic tensions, often hinders the call to be united with the other in Christ, with those who do not look like me. But as Beth Stovell reminds us, there is no "other. There is only us."[12]

Israel's experience informs its call to be hospitable to foreigners. A key theological theme in Leviticus and Deuteronomy is the idea that Israel should care for *them* because they are actually *us*. The foreigner is a picture of who Israel was at an earlier stage of its story, and this moves the foreigner from a distant other to a familiar us. This shift from *them* to *us* characterizes the eschatological visions we find in the New Testament, showing us God's ultimate vision for his people. This informs how we live out God's kingdom in the world today through hospitality and hope, creating a biblical theological foundation for diaspora ministry.[13]

Michael Bird writes of something similar from the Rwanda genocide:

> The history of the church provides numerous impressive testimonies of the power of the gospel to break down the wall of separation between different races and cultures. One of the most remarkable stories of this kind from recent history emerged from the bloody conflict in Rwanda, where in 1994 members of the Hutu tribe carried out mass murders of the Tutsi tribes. At the town of Ruhanga, fifteen kilometers outside Kigali, a group of 13,500 Christians had gathered for refuge. They were of various denominations: Anglicans, Roman Catholics, Pentecostals, Baptists, and others. According to the account of a witness to the scene, "When the militias came, they ordered the Hutus and Tutsis to separate themselves by tribe. The people refused and declared that they were all one in Christ, and for that they were all killed," gunned down *en masse* and dumped into mass graves. It is a disturbing story, but it is also a compelling witness to the power of the gospel to overcome ethnic division. Paul would have regarded these Rwanda martyrs as faithful witnesses to the truth of the gospel.

> Having been "crucified with Christ," they preferred to die rather than to deny the grace of God that had made them one in Christ.[14]

The influx of refugees and immigrants into countries that were previously their colonisers has created major ethnic challenges and tensions throughout the world. The refugee situation is unlikely to get better anytime soon. The world is experiencing a refugee crisis, with millions of people being forced to flee their home countries due to conflict or violence, or in search of a better future. The number of displaced people is at an all-time high. Estimates at June 2023 ran at 110,000,000 displaced people.[15]

Whilst it is so that the refugee crisis means that border controls and immigration in most countries will be tightened and will need to be managed responsibly, what is the response of the Church to displaced peoples? As I type this on 27/01/2025, it is in the aftermath of the USA having deported hundreds of illegal immigrants back to Columbia, Brazil, Panama, and more. Whilst being respectful of Nation State sovereignty, and the need to control migration in a humane way, a question still emerges: *what is the Church's response to this humanitarian crisis?* Caesar does what Caesar does dependent on who the ruling Caesar of the day is. Some Caesars, of course, are more humane than others. The question, though, is posed to the Church. The twofold call of every Old Testament prophet, to return to God and look after those who cannot look after themselves, is as relevant now as then, when the prophets called for care of the poor, orphans, widows, and aliens. Those categories still exist, and we might add to them those who are trafficked for labour or into the sex trade and more.

Immigration is having a profound effect on countries like Canada. According to the 2016 Census of Population, more than 7.5 million foreign-born people from two hundred countries reside in Canada. Statistics Canada predicts that by 2036, immigrants will represent 30 percent of Canada's total population. The same report suggests that in less than twenty years, immigrants and second-generation individuals could represent between 44 and 50 percent of the nation's population. Immigration waves into Canada had in the past come largely from Europe. Most immigrants now come from the Middle East, Asia, and Africa. These new residents arrive with their languages, cultures, and religions intact. Approximately half of these new Canadians are Christian.[16] As the church of Jesus Christ, it would be remiss of us not to embrace and welcome our brothers and sisters as they seek to be part of communities of faith in their own languages and in their own styles of worship. It would be equally short-sighted not to consider the missional and evangelistic task at hand for the Church regarding the new Canadians who are of different faiths. Embracing new Canadians must mean more than sharing our buildings, resources and facilities. Hospitality needs a radical edge to it in the times in which we live.

> Caesar does what Caesar does dependent on who the ruling Caesar of the day is. Some Caesars, of course, are more humane than others.

My country of origin, South Africa, is in many ways to Africa what the USA, Canada, and Europe are to the rest of the world. It is a perceived place of safety, opportunity, and respite for a fleeing diaspora. Oftentimes there is a significant gap between what is perceived and reality. In casual conversations with followers of Jesus from the Global North, regardless of their country of origin, it is concerning how much of our conversation around the global refugee crisis is more concerned with border control, stricter immigration policies, safety, and protection than care of the "orphan, the widow, and the alien." Immigration controls and border protection are certainly important. Nation States do need to protect their sovereignty and the safety of their citizens. But we are faced with a humanitarian crisis of enormous proportion and the fleeing diaspora are seeking security, opportunity and a better future, as we all are. *Bigger Things* is less concerned with the response of individual nation states to the refugee crisis than with the response of the Church to the foreigner who enters their country. The twofold call of the Old Testament prophets, which was echoed by John the Baptist and Jesus, remains: return to God and look after those who are unable to look after themselves.

In missions circles it is quite common to hear people pray for the nations. "Lord, would you give us the nations!" Yet when the nations are brought to our doorstep, do we sing a different tune?

PRAYER RESPONSE

Tongues are magnificent, thank you Lord! A Church that hosts the nations is even greater. More bigger things please Jesus. We asked for the nations. You gave us the nations. Teach us to care for the nations who you brought to our doorstep.

CHAPTER 2

"LET HE AMONG YOU"

"Courage is grace under pressure."

ERNEST HEMINGWAY

During my time with the Anglican parish of St. John's Wynberg in Cape Town, I was seconded to St. Barnabas Church Kloof Nek Road, Cape Town. The parishes of St. John's and St. Barnabas were partnering in what was to be a church implant. I always felt the term church implant sounded like a prosthetic limb rather than a ministry. Nonetheless, this is what it was called.

Harry Wiggett was the outgoing priest at St. Barnabas. Harry is a character of some note and a very well-known and beloved author, speaker and poet who still lives and writes from a suburb called Fish Hoek in Cape Town. Harry, in his own words, often said that he had been sent to St. Barnabas to preside over the death of a church. About two years prior to his retirement, he reached out to the evangelical and charismatic parish of the six churches in the St. John's network to see if there was any opportunity for cooperation toward a renewal ministry of some kind. The net result was that a team of three leaders, along with a group of thirty so-called implanted volunteer members, was sent from St. John's Parish to St. Barnabas.

The team lead was Peter Holgate, who was a mentor of mine and had been a lecturer at the Cornerstone Institute where I completed my undergraduate studies. Peter was a bit of a legend in evangelical circles in Cape Town, having been prominent in Scripture Union and the director of China Inland Mission (now Overseas Missionary Fellowship) in South Africa. Aside from that, Peter was a gentleman of a bygone era and a thoroughly decent individual. Peter invited me to be part of the leadership team as the assistant pastor and church planter. I accepted and was employed and sent by the parish of St. John's Wynberg. The other member of our team of three was Christian Senyoni, a refugee to South Africa from the 1994 Rwanda genocide. Christian and I were good friends from our Cornerstone days. Christian now resides and ministers as a priest in the Episcopal Church of the USA. Under Peter's lead, the team of three and our families, along with about twenty to thirty volunteers, implanted a team that effectively doubled the size of St. Barnabas.

By the time we arrived at St. Barnabas, Harry was in his last year of pastoral ministry prior to retirement. He asked us to allow him to see his ministry out in the way he was accustomed to doing it and for us to build "fresh expressions" around the traditional Anglican expression of *Eucharisto* without removing anything that was already in place. It was during the St. Barnabas years that I came to appreciate the full diversity of differing expressions of the faith that were not better or worse than other expressions, but simply different. What was accomplished at Barneys, as it was fondly called, was in fact quite profound.

The early morning traditional Sunday Eucharist was still conducted from the original *Thomas Cranmer Anglican Prayer Book* of 1549, more often called the *Book of Common Prayer*. To this we later added a freer family service that gathered at 10:00am on Sundays, used a far more modern prayer book, and included contemporary worship music. After a little more time had passed, we added a charismatic evening service that was under my care. We ran numerous Alpha courses, prayed on the streets of Cape Town, and partnered with both our Dutch Reformed Neighbours from Tamboerskloof Dutch Reformed Church and with the City Vineyard who rented premises from us. It was here that I was properly introduced to the Vineyard movement, although I had interacted with them previously.

The rate of Alpha attendees becoming disciples of Jesus in that five-year period is unmatched by anything I had seen before or have seen since. The church was growing by conversion rather than transfer growth. Over five or six years, Barneys grew to nearly two hundred souls spread across three Sunday worship services. We built an additional ultra-modern ministry and office block onto what was an historical Herbert Baker designed stone Anglican building. The building won an architectural design award for the year in which it was completed.

To the best of my knowledge, Barneys still flourishes as a significant Anglican congregation in the heart of Cape Town. The five years I spent in ministry at St. Barnabas were some of the best, and some of the worst, of my life. The work remains though, and many others have built on the renewal work that was done in the early 2000s. The foundational work had been done a century or more prior. Our work was not foundational, rather it was the work of renewal. As Paul says in 1 Corinthians 3:6 (NIV), "I planted the seed, Apollos watered it, but God has been making it grow." We are instruments in God's hands and the personalities involved are not of any lasting significance, despite the personality cults we may witness in the Church in the world currently. It really is down to God. In hindsight, what was accomplished in that small Anglican church was in every way a bigger thing. There were many battles won and many lost along the way. I highlight a few such stories below.

The architect's model of the modern addition to the traditional Herbert Baker Table Mountain Sand-stone Church. The additions are seen on the far right.

The day I reported for duty at Barneys I had not yet met Harry Wiggett. I arrived at the church early on a Monday morning and tried to get inside. Everything was locked so I knocked and shouted. Eventually a skinny priest of average height with protruding teeth, dressed in cassock and surplus, with a frightfully English accent, popped his head over the perimeter wall. He said "Oh you must be Melt! I believe you want to be an Anglican priest!' My response was something like, "Harry, I am not at all sure that I want to be an Anglican priest, time will tell, but in the meantime I'm here to do work for the Kingdom of God." Harry replied, "Oh good, good, because in fact anyone can be an Anglican priest, even a parrot, but the only thing the parrot can't do is hold the cup!" That was my introduction to the inimitable Harry Wiggett.

Our first few years at St. Barnabas were hard. Coming out of fifteen years in the corporate world where I had recently begun earning well, these years were financially strenuous for my family. The Anglican Diocese of Table Bay seemed oblivious of how we struggled. There was also significant resistance from a few of the parishioners regarding what we had been sent to do. There was clearly unexpressed dissatisfaction from the largely liberal Diocese of Table Bay that St. Barnabas had partnered with the evangelical and charismatic grouping of Anglicans from within their ranks. Anyone reading this who has navigated similar Anglican waters will likely have some understanding of what we faced.

The evening on which I attended my first St. Barnabas parish council meeting was interesting. I introduced myself to an older lady named Olga. Olga had in her younger days run four-hundred-meter hurdles for the Dutch national team at the Olympic games. She was as tough as old boot leather. On introducing myself to her, I recall asking what she did in the church. She gave me an ice-cold glare and said, "I am the official opposition." Olga, although remaining confrontational and even obnoxious at times, became a wonderful and caring partner in the renewal and fresh expressions of St. Barnabas as trust levels grew amongst the team and the church.

My personal struggles and indeed significant disillusionment from those years does not detract from what God accomplished, both in me and at St. Barnabas. The Anglican ordinands programme I came into with a view to join the priesthood was contrived, and in many ways bloody-minded, at that time. That, along with the financial pressure we were under and St. John's rehousing our young family four times in five years, proved to be my eventual undoing. I never saw the process through to the priesthood and moved tribal loyalty to the Vineyard. I remember hearing God whisper that I had moved from trying to fulfil a call I felt I had heard, to proving a point in that I would be priested come hell or high water. To retain my integrity, I needed to move on, so I did.

I remain grateful for the St. Barnabas years in which we truly saw God's Spirit move and God's Kingdom come in every way imaginable to us at the time. We witnessed multiple deliverances, conversions, salvation, healings, and more. I started meeting with one young medical student in her parents' home on Wednesday evenings. That group grew to a small group of over ten young University of Cape Town students. The most significant individual bigger thing I can recall from those years is not a story relating to St. Barnabas directly. It is a story about the inimitable Harry Wiggett. And it is a story of a bigger thing worth telling.

Harry was in every way a riddle wrapped in an enigma. Fairly liberal and Anglo-Catholic in his theology, of his own volition, he sought out a group of Anglican charismatics to partner with. The man had some imagination for the Kingdom! In true Anglican fashion he was able to be all things to all people. Just when you thought he was one thing, he showed himself to be another. A part of his life story as an Anglican priest was that he was Nelson Mandela's priest. He features in the biography on Mandela's life, *Long Walk to Freedom*. Harry served Mandela communion every week for several years when Mandela was imprisoned in Pollsmoor Prison. Harry has been called one of the unsung heroes of South Africa. *Someone very famous once said that true prophets are seldom recognised in their home countries.* Mandela recounted how it was Harry who led him to understand why there are four Gospels in the New Testament rather than one.[17]

In the 1980s when apartheid was at its zenith, one of Harry's Anglican placements was in the towns of Ceres and Tulbagh, in the beautiful winelands of the western Cape in the Tulbagh basin. The basin is fringed on three sides by mountains and drained by the Klein Berg River and its tributaries. Harry was the priest at the Anglican church and served that community in the early 1980s, at the time when anti-apartheid demonstrations and political turmoil were running rife through South Africa. One day, Harry was driving home from church in his VW Beetle, still in his clerical garb from presiding over the Sunday morning Eucharist service. He drove right into the middle of a group of demonstrators and decided to take a detour down an alley he thought would be a shortcut home. The alley turned out to be a cul-de-sac. At the end of the cul-de-sac were four Black men. Three were brandishing spears and bricks, and one was a cowering uniformed policeman. The most despised people in South Africa at that time might well have been Black Africans who worked for the South African Police (SAP), who were regarded as sellouts by their own people.

The three men armed with bricks and spears were literally about to kill the cornered police officer. Harry somehow managed to squeeze his VW Beetle between the attackers and the target. He climbed out of his car and onto the bonnet. It is worth noting that Harry Wiggett, fully robed in cassock, surplus, stole and whatever else, soaking wet could not weigh more than 65 kilograms. Once on the bonnet, he raised his arms into the air and shouted: "Stop, stop, stop! Let him among you who is without sin cast the first stone." One by one the African men lowered their spears, dropped their bricks, and walked off, leaving the policeman and Harry unharmed.

PRAYER RESPONSE

Bigger things. Just way, way bigger things. Could we have more of these in our troubled times, please Lord? We need you.

CHAPTER 3

BIBLICAL AUTHORITY AND THE NEED TO INTERPRET

"The broader problem is that a great deal of popular preaching and teaching uses the Bible as a pegboard on which to hang a fair bit of Christianised pop-psychology or moralising encouragement, with very little effort to teach the faithful, from the Bible, the massive doctrines of historic, confessional Christianity."

D.A. CARSON

The inclusion of a chapter on hermeneutics could seem a little ambitious in a book of this nature and scope. There is, after all, a prolific amount of literature available on reading and interpreting Scripture responsibly. One of the most accessible is Douglas Stuart's and Gordon D. Fee's *How to Read the Bible for All Its Worth*.[18]

There are several resources the reader could consult for an in-depth approach to reading and using the Bible sensibly, responsibly and indeed prophetically. The aim with this chapter is not to replace a college or seminary course on hermeneutics in any way. Rather, it is to express Vineyard's posture toward these things. At best, this chapter is an overview with some handles to consider when approaching the Scriptures with a view to their responsible use, rather than their wholesale abuse, of which there has been too much over the years.

In my own journey, I am grateful to have come from more traditionally interpretation-focused churches into more charismatic environments. I had already been schooled in biblical interpretation in more conservative environments when I started asking questions about how a consistent hermeneutic suddenly changed its interpretive approach when it came to the things of the Spirit in Scripture. Doing modules in systematics as an MTh major in 2004 and 2005 was also immensely helpful.

> Biblical theology is no longer popularly in vogue and we are collectively much poorer for it.

Landing in Vineyard in 2006 was a coming together of the two worlds I wanted to inhabit: what was called at the time "the quest for the radical middle"[19] on the continuum of Word and Spirit. So many others like Vineyard existed then and exist now, but for me, a world in which the move of God's Spirit was taken as seriously as biblical interpretation was new. I always have been and remain unconvinced that the polarity of a continuum is the best way to describe a union of Word and Spirit. I would prefer to speak of it as a fusion that could be illustrated by a DNA strand where blue is Word and red is Spirit.

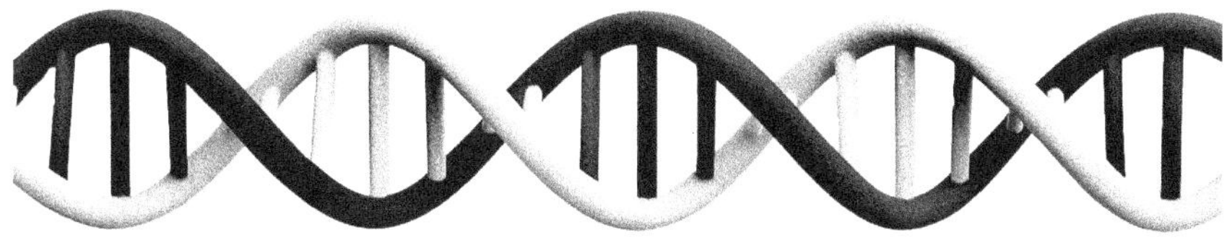

A few years ago, I described Vineyard churches in this way:

> Some are revivalist and others are not particularly so. A new generation of Vineyard leaders has emerged to some of whom these things are ancient history and not of much interest. But no matter the differences in individual emphasis, there are certain things that are common and dear to all Vineyard churches. These are the values around which we, as one small group of the broader Church of Jesus Christ, gather. Vineyard is at root a kingdom-seeking, redemptive, missionary and church planting movement with a deep desire for intimate worship of God in music. Our way of belonging is best expressed in a centred set. We long for biblical justice and express that longing in ministry and advocacy amongst the poor, the dispossessed, the powerless and the marginalized. Our theology rests in the ancient creeds, such as the Nicene and Apostles' Creeds, interpreted through the lenses of the coming of the Kingdom. We seek to live in the radical middle between the coming of the Kingdom and its eventual consummation. We continue to try to do only what we see the Father doing, which can be difficult to discern, but is a worthy goal, nonetheless. We work toward healing and wholeness ministered through prayer with the expectation of the nearness of the Kingdom, but without the triumphalism

> vested in an over-realised eschatology. *We are in varying degrees ecumenical, evangelical (in the original sense), contemplative, and Pentecostal.* We continue to try to follow the lasting thoughts of our founder John Wimber to "take the best and to run with it," and to be a perpetually self-renewing organization...continuous renewal is our heritage and for many of us, continually on our hearts.[20]

At times in our history, we likely erred in our quest for the radical middle as we mistook signs and wonders as the Kingdom itself, rather than as signs that pointed to the coming of the Kingdom. David Ruis said it like this at our 2018 national gathering:

> Another dynamic was that of a subtle waning away of robust equipping, teaching, and engaged learning. There was a growing posture of waiting for the "silver bullet"—the "word"—the extraordinary breaking in of tangible manifestations of God's presence that started to be not only a signpost of the kingdom upon us, but a belief that this was actually the kingdom itself. If the healing didn't come, the kingdom hadn't come. If the breakthrough didn't come, the kingdom didn't come. If the feathers didn't fall, or the gold didn't appear, the anointing was gone. Like addicts constantly needing another "hit," another "fix" for a better high, a better experience, we too began to be addicted.[21]

As the charismatic edge of the Vineyard movement pushed harder and more insistently into the supernatural,[22] more balanced voices within have drawn us back toward the centre to the extent that some *now feel we have over-corrected.* The goal of *Bigger Things* is to draw us back toward a balanced centre that continues to pray and long for the Holy Spirit's deep and authentic presence amongst us, whilst using the

Scriptures faithfully, sensibly, and carefully. These two things are by no means diametrically opposed to one another. At their best expression, *in combination*, they might be as close as anything else to fully living the Kingdom life that is available to us now.

What follows will be a basic framework for using Scripture responsibly, and indeed at times prophetically, without falling into some of the more bizarre imaginings that have emerged from a radically over-realised eschatology.

THE META-NARRATIVE ARC OF CREATION

The Christian story or narrative arc of Scripture comprises Creation, Fall, Sin, Redeemer, Redemption, ***Parousia*** and Consummation. When dealing with a text, it is always useful as an opening consideration to determine where we are in the big story, the grand narrative of Scripture.

> ***Parousia*** is the time when Jesus Christ returns physically to earth to judge creation and humanity and to consummate his Kingdom.

The essence of Scripture is captured in the Apostles' and Nicene Creeds, which summarize its meta-narrative. These creeds offer a bird's eye view of the Bible's story. Rob Bell notes that "When we read the Bible, we can study a verse, reflect on a sentence, explore the flow of several verses, or study a paragraph or chapter. But we can also fly higher and look at the entire book. The Bible is best understood as a cohesive story, with its individual parts gaining fuller meaning within the larger picture."[23]

In 2021, I had just completed a doctoral project. A woman in our congregation, who I will call Rubie, asked if she could read it. From 150 pages of reading, she lifted out just one quote:

> There are a few possible restrictions around the call to radical diversity and inclusivity. After a two-year listening exercise, AVC Canada has landed back in the traditionally orthodox biblical understanding of marriage being between one man and one woman. Everyone is welcome to worship in Vineyard churches, but not everyone is able to serve in leadership roles. The guide contains position papers along with other tools to help AVC navigate LBGTQ2+ issues and articulate our collective response. *The emergence of sexual identifiers previously unknown to us, such as gender fluidity, means that sexual identity ought to be regarded as an ongoing conversation.* I believe that we should never tightly define our position on any of these discussions. There are *identifiers being adopted by various people now of which the Scriptures are completely unaware and therefore completely silent.* The need for a guide toward an orderly and articulated navigation of our typically Vineyard "middle of the road" position on LBGTQ2+ is clear. This will help prevent further conflict

> when situations requiring a disciplinary process arise, as they already have, and as they most certainly will in the future.[24]

Despite the quote reflecting Vineyard Canada as landing in an orthodox Scriptural interpretation as it relates to marriage, I received a scathing email from Rubie saying there ought to be no discussion on these things at all since God has already spoken absolutely. I asked her where it was that God has spoken *absolutely* about gender confusion in Scripture. She quoted Genesis 1:27 (NIV), "male and female he created them." I asked her in which chapter of Genesis it was that humanity fell into sin. She was unable to answer, but for clarity it is Genesis 3, two chapters after the verse she quoted as *absolute*. I mentioned that she was quoting a text located in a perfect world before sin had entered creation. I asked whether we were allowed to discuss gossip, greed, fear, or any other sin or brokenness and she replied, "of course!" I confess that my response could have been much more gracious. I replied, "By your reasoning human sexuality was somehow miraculously protected in the fall. By that same reasoning you and I should be sitting naked in the garden, discussing this and feeling no shame." Rubie scuttled off to a different church in the city and has not contacted me again. I am biblically orthodox as it relates to marriage. But I know that there are no easy, one verse, cherry picked answers to extremely complex questions. That recognition tends not to sit particularly well with either theological fundamentalists or theological progressives.

> There is some irony in the fact that theological liberals and theological conservatives both seem to want similar, albeit totally opposite, responses to complex questions. A simply defined, black or white answer to extraordinarily complex questions in a world that comes to us in shades of grey.

Shades of grey often lead us to make the choice between two apparently equally valid and equally biblically based arguments. The care of an unborn infant versus a woman's right to care for her body and make her own choices, as example, regardless of our own personal convictions, could both be argued with significant biblically based reasoning. Occasionally, shades of grey force us to choose the "least bad" option. For example, political elections might leave us with two candidates we regard as equally unqualified. Doctors must sometimes choose between saving the life of an infant or that of the mother. Although rare now, there was a time when doctors were quite often forced to make this choice during childbirth. The complexity of life seldom offers us the luxury of clearly defined binary options.

> Aside from holding to biblical orthodoxy in marriage, I also hold to biblical orthodoxy in terms of whom Jesus and Scripture in general calls me to love. From the Gospels to the Epistles, it would seem to include everyone. Every human bears the image of God. It is the image of God in all of humanity that makes everyone my neighbour. "My neighbour" cannot exclude the neighbours who disagree with me or live a lifestyle of which I do not approve (John 13:34-35, 2 Cor 5:16). The parable of the Good Samaritan makes the point that my neighbour is exactly the person I had hoped my neighbour would not be.

If Rubie had been willing to have a conversation rather than shutting me down, and if I had been a little less sarcastic and shirty in my response to her, perhaps the outcome could have looked different, although I doubt it. Rubie seemed unwilling to consider *where in the story we were* and so her interpretation made little sense to anyone interested in context at all. The next topic we need to cover is *biblical authority* and what that means.

BIBLICAL AUTHORITY

Biblical authority is both an important and a contested concept. What do we mean when we say the Bible has authority? Do the words standing alone have authority? Does every interpretation have authority? Does it have authority on every subject or is the Bible's authority limited to "religious" concepts? This section addresses these questions, with some sociological and psychological concepts thrown in for good measure.

Most Christians believe that the Bible has great authority. It does introduce us to Jesus, after all. Believers do not necessarily use the same words to describe that authority, but they are at least in agreement that the Bible does indeed have, in the original evangelical sense, *authority unto faith and life.* But how does this authority work? We need to get our minds around what this authority is if we want to be able to use the Scriptures without confusion. Whatever you have been taught about biblical authority, for good or ill, at this point, let's try to *reimagine* it together. The aim is to come away with just the essence of what that might look like.

2 Timothy 3:16-17 (NIV) says "All Scripture is God-breathed (***theopneustos***) and is useful for teaching, rebuking, correcting, and training in righteousness, so that the servant of God may be thoroughly equipped for every good work." Essentially, recognising that Scripture has authority would be our combined affirmation that the Bible is God's *written word to you and me for us to see and taste that Jesus is good and that Jesus is Lord.* And this is so, regardless of our tradition, location, or context. The Bible is authoritative because it is God's primary—certainly not exclusive, but primary—means of self-disclosure. There

are two extreme and equally faulty views regarding biblical authority that many followers of Jesus routinely hold to. One is called moral therapeutic deism, which is when people believe the Scriptures are there just to *make me feel a little better about myself.* I fully understand how people land here. There have been dreadful machinations of Scripture, supposedly prophetic and otherwise, that have used and abused it most irresponsibly. We need to be honest about these things. Scripture has been used to justify and promote slavery, oppression, patriarchy, women submitting to all sorts of sexual abuses because of so-called male headship, and more. We really need to be able to be honest about these things.

***Theopneustos* (θεοπνευστος)** is a Greek word that means "God-breathed" or divinely inspired. Theos **(θεος)** means God and the verb **πνεω** is to breathe or to "blow out." In that sense, the Scriptures are breathed out by God, but penned by human authors.

Moral therapeutic deism is one extreme and one wrong way of viewing the Scriptures. The other extreme is an overt focus on the Scriptures that ends up becoming an end in and of itself. In that way, the Bible becomes the thing that we worship instead of the Bible pointing us to the one whom we worship. That posture could be called bibliolatry, and it is rife within conservative expressions of the faith. Used in this way we can end up thinking more highly of the Bible than we do of the God whom the Bible reveals to us. Though it is true that some believers have deserted any commitment to Scripture as authoritative in any significant way, we need to acknowledge that at the other extreme there is an equal but quite different problem.

It is almost certain that it is the churches who can hold the tension of the culture wars and more without falling to either fundamentalism or wholesale progressivism who will be the *guardians of the orthodoxy of the faith* in these dreadfully divisive times. ***Orthodoxy*** is used throughout the book as indicating those things that have been regarded as *the essential tenets of our faith* over centuries. This to distinguish its use from Eastern Orthodoxy as a branch of the Universal Church that split from the Western churches in the Great Schism of 1054.

> ***Biblical orthodoxy*** is the acceptance of the doctrines and creeds of the Christian faith based on the Bible and the ancient Church councils. The term orthodoxy comes from the Greek words orthos meaning right, straight, or true **(ορθος)** and doxa **(δοξα)** meaning notion, opinion or judgement. Literally translated it is right worship, in the sense of holding a right opinion on matters of the faith.

Let's talk a little more about what we do and do not mean by the term biblical authority. There are three main points through which we will approach the term:

1. Differentiating where and when Scripture is *prescriptive* and where and when it is merely *descriptive.* Or as Beth Stovell writes, "not every text [is] instructing us to go and do likewise."[25] Abram's call to sacrifice Isaac is not prescriptive for you and me. Nor is David's adulterous affair with Bathsheba. Those are *descriptive* texts.
2. Going, as the ancient creeds do, beyond Scripture to responsibly interpret Scripture.
3. What it ultimately is that makes the Bible authoritative.[26]

To start this discussion, I will share a slightly incendiary comment: Scripture is not the Christian's highest authority. The Triune God who is most fully known *through the Scriptures* is our highest authority. The Triune God who speaks through the Scriptures—but not exclusively—is our highest authority. The God who brings us from an illuminated reading of the Scriptures to the feet of Jesus, through the Holy Spirit, is our ultimate authority.

The Westminster Confession of Faith says that "the Holy Spirit is the supreme judge of all things." The Holy Spirit is our ultimate authority whether through Scripture, dreams and visions, prophecy, nature, music, relationship, or in whatever other means he chooses to reveal Jesus to us. It should be extremely encouraging to the Vineyard or any other Spirit movement, that a reformed confession—the Westminster Confession—communicates that ultimate authority resides in communal discernment by the Holy Spirit.

If this line of reasoning is followed, things like prophecy, words of wisdom and knowledge, prompts, dreams, the arts, music, nature, visions, pictures, and indeed the application of Scripture and more, are to be examined in community by none other than the Holy Spirit. Scripture is not inherently authoritative because of its teaching, or power, or because it contains some kind of magical formulae. Scripture is authoritative because the Holy Spirit speaks through it predominantly and it is the Holy Spirit who is our ultimate authority. And if it is the Holy Spirit who speaks in Scripture, then the authority of Scripture needs to be anchored into ***pneumatology***. The recognition that the authority of Scripture is anchored into pneumatology makes us, in *every thoroughly right sense*, a charismatic people.

Pneumatology is the study of the Holy Spirit in Christian theology. The word comes from the Greek word ***pneuma* (πνευμα)** which means breath or spirit. It is a branch of Christian systematic theology.

When one reads the Great Commissions in the Gospels, we find that Jesus did not say, "all authority in heaven and earth is given to the books you mangey lot will write about me." He says, "all authority in heaven and earth is given to me" (Matt 28:18, NIV). He goes on to bestow that same authority on his followers. We land in a place then where the preached word is somehow the word of God, nature is somehow the word of God according to Paul, our Lectio readings are the word of God, prophecy is the word of God. But all these things only *become the authoritative word of God* when they are interpreted and weighed by the Holy Spirit and all of them are pointers to the ultimate and incarnate Word of God—Jesus.

> It is our Holy Spirit inspired encounters with Jesus, through and by Scripture and whatever other means, which then become authoritative.

Authority comes by God's Spirit speaking through the preached Word, the Lectio, the reading. Through the inductive or deductive Bible Study. God's Spirit speaking through the prophesy, the prompt, the picture, or nature, or whatever. Once we receive those encounters as revelatory of Jesus,[27] they become, for us, *authoritative.* Scripture is the predominant space in which we encounter Jesus by the Spirit. Scripture is therefore authoritative. In the North Americas in 2025, there are many churches that place an extremely high view on biblical authority with scarcely a mention of the Holy Spirit. Where there is no Holy Spirit inspired, Christo-centric lens through which to interpret Scripture, we end up in bibliolatry.

That would be where we potentially go "stupid." It is in this kind of space where we end up reading *description as prescription.* It is where we read a grace-based passage in the New Testament as if we are reading the Levitical holiness code to ancient Israel. The Bible is not authoritative because it contains magic, or the ***Gnostic*** thinking evident in secret knowledge—"I know things that you don't know."[28] The Bible is authoritative because in our reading of it we discover that Jesus is the Christ, the Messiah, the anointed one of God and he finds us on the pages of the Bible and we find him there too. From Genesis to the Revelation, the Bible is authoritative because it contains the self-disclosure of the Triune God. The Bible then is authoritative, but it is not even close to being *consistently prescriptive.*

Gnosticism is a prominent movement that grew between the second (or late first) and fifth centuries. It grew concurrent with the growth of the Early Church and was a continuous challenge in the Church. It is an eclectic teaching of many things with some common threads. It sees creation as inherently bad and spirit as good.

PRESCRIPTION VERSUS DESCRIPTION IN SCRIPTURE

Much of the biblical story describes things that happened historically. This type of writing is called historical narrative. These are things recorded for posterity in the canon of Scripture, but they are not injunctions for us to follow. There are numerous recordings like this in the Bible. The stories of a plethora of conflicts and the wars of all the Old Testament kings are such texts. David's sin with Bathsheba, Abram effectively pimping out his wife to Pharoah (Gen 12), Jacob stealing his brother's birthright, the strong hints that Noah was raped homosexually in his drunkenness (Gen 9),[29] Ananias and Saphira's lies (Acts 5:1-11), and so many more, are recorded for us. However, at least one would think, no one with their mental faculties intact interprets or suggests that these are texts which are *meant to be emulated by us.*

Yet—bizarre as this may seem to any rational thinking follower of Jesus—we are faced with interpretations of Scripture now that read descriptions of the wars between Ancient Israel and the Canaanites and other biblical peoples as *prescriptive.* This "interpretation" then results, on occasion, in a demonically inspired "solution" to the current Israel/Palestine conflict. How in heaven and on earth did we get here? In a violent world, we get sucked all too easily into a vision for the Kingdom wherein, in the words of Leonard Sweet, "the instrument (of God's hand) can quickly take the form of a whip to beat God's will into people."[30]

> Victory through violence. Yet that is not how Jesus' kingdom will come. The kingdom will come rather, through the imperial violence done to him on the cross, and through the anti-imperial, death reversing, justice loving power of the resurrection. Then, the kingdom spreads, not through conquest, but through the Spirit's life giving and liberating

> power being experienced by more and more people and through their life-giving contributions to the world.[31]

Fairly recently, like many of you, I watched the election debate between Biden and Trump, prior to Kamala Harris being a late replacement for the Democrats. The debate was akin to two soft brained, testosterone fueled adolescent boys having it out on a school playground. Biden accused Trump of having the morals of an alley cat and Trump bragged about his golf handicap. Seriously? These are the so-called leaders of the free world. Whatever happened to a bygone era of statesmanship and gentleperson like conduct? These people—world leaders—should be ashamed of themselves. Our challenge is that the aggressive, sneering, smug gloating and reprehensible behaviour on display in the political sphere has been adopted by not just a few in the Church of Jesus Christ. Some Church leaders seem impressed by this kind of rhetoric as a show of strength. How can this be? The only thing it shows me is a lack of character, and how deep the excrement we are in might be. The Apostle Paul reminds us, "but the fruit of the Spirit is love, joy, peace, patience, kindness, goodness, faithfulness, gentleness, and self-control" (Gal 5:22-23, ESV). None of this is evident in these politicians, and yet, some high-profile Christian leaders are applauding and emulating this shameful conduct from the margins.

Some of the narrative sections of *Bigger Things* will likely not date too well with the pace of change—particularly in the political sphere—that is upon us. I share them as current to the time in which I am writing, recognising a challenge I do not quite know how to overcome. Yet I am prayerful that the application and insights can stretch beyond current circumstances.

In 1995, John Wimber spoke of the fundamentalist spirit of combat that sweepingly condemns anything it fails to understand, which would seem to be most things:

> Our society at large has succumbed to a spirit of rudeness, vitriol and put down…we are rapidly becoming a society of fearful people pitted against each other, along racial, political and economic lines…both sides use pejorative language to paint with broad brush strokes, the failings of the other side. Our culture glorifies rudeness.[32]

As a former competitive rugby player, and avid rugby supporter, I watch Six Nations, United rugby Championship, and Major League Rugby matches, while most of the North Americas watch other sports. Today, watching Scotland versus France at *Stade de France* (15/03/2025), one of the commentators summed up the disillusionment of many when a scuffle broke out between the French and Scots. He said, "come on fellows, this is a rugby match, not the Oval Office." Shame on them. The politicians I mean, not the rugby players. Shame, shame, shame on them. They are paid public servants. Someone needs to remind them that they are there to serve.

> In large part the theological task is, and always has been, to discern and determine which parts of the Bible are limited to the culture they address and which parts transcend culture. That is the primary task of active interpretation.

As a quick exercise of interpreting Galatians 5:22-23 then, clearly the fruit of the Spirit is not culturally located. It is for all followers of Jesus in all ages. All followers of Jesus are meant to display the fruit of the Spirit in all times.

MOVING BEYOND SCRIPTURE TO RESPONSIBLY INTERPRET SCRIPTURE

The most obvious example of moving outside of Scripture to interpret Scripture responsibly is the formulation of Trinity. Nowhere in the Bible does the word Trinity appear. In fact, nowhere in the Bible does the Greek word which we use to describe Trinity—or more accurately, to describe the relationship between Jesus and the Father—***homoousios*** (ὀμοουσιος), appear.[33]

> ***Homoousios*** **(ὀμοουσιος)** is a theological term that describes the relationship between Jesus Christ and God the Father as being of the same essence or substance. It is a word that helps us clarify the relationship between Father and Son.

The word is not found anywhere in Scripture, but it is used in the Nicene Creed to describe the relationship between the Father and the Son: "of the same essence as the Father." Trinitarian formulations are not found in Scripture, but they are summarised in the ancient creeds. The credal formulations, in a sense, go beyond Scripture in order to responsibly interpret Scripture. The doctrine of the Trinity is found in Scripture, but not by name. It is the result of a hermeneutical process. The drawing out of the doctrine that is in Scripture then ends up in the credal formulations as the best way we have of describing the God who we worship. Even though these words do not appear in Scripture, they are an essential aspect of our faith if we are to remain within historical orthodoxy. Trinitarian formulation is a way of articulating what the Scriptures affirm about the triune nature of the Godhead. The formulations protect us from various extremes.

Without these formulations that go beyond Scripture to land in an orthodox interpretation of Scripture, it is almost inevitable that we will land in ***adoptionism***, ***subordinationism***, or ***modalism***.[34] The historical creeds in general are the result of a hermeneutical process. Tell that to a fundamentalist and you might hear that the doctrine of the Trinity dropped, carved on stone tablets, from the heavenlies. But that is not true. It is not even close to true. The credal statements are, in general, interpretations and summaries of the main themes of Scripture. I affirm these things because over more than two thousand years the collective response of the Church to these things has been affirmation. *We receive the faith as it is handed down to us*,[35] and we trust that the Holy Spirit has ministered collectively to his people over centuries. These things are all there to help us navigate what Todd Rutkowski calls the "maze of Scripture."[36] These things help us understand and use the Scriptures responsibly, faithfully and with great reverence and care. They help us make sense of the fact that there is one God who has revealed himself in three equally divine persons.

> The credal formulations, in a sense, go beyond Scripture in order to responsibly interpret Scripture. The doctrine of the Trinity is found in Scripture, but not by name. It is the result of a hermeneutical process.

Adoptionism is also called ***dynamic Monarchianism***. It is a non-trinitarian doctrine that holds to Jesus being adopted as the Son of God at his baptism or resurrection.

Subordinationism teaches Trinity as a hierarchy rather than as having co-equal divinity in perfect relational harmony. In this view, which is not uncommon, the Son and the Holy Spirit are eternally subordinate to the Father. It has significant outworking on ministry and life.

Modalism is the belief that God reveals himself in three modes, or forms, rather than as three distinct persons. Some of the common illustrations preachers tend to use to try and explain Trinity lean into this kind of thought.

THE NEW TESTAMENT AS MESSIANIC INTERPRETATION OF THE OLD TESTAMENT

Richard B. Hayes was a beloved and immensely gifted New Testament scholar from Duke Divinity School in Durham, North Carolina. He passed away early in 2025. In his book *Reading Backwards*, he argues that reading the Bible backwards is the only way of reading it if we truly wish to gain an understanding of it.[37] He explains, "Only by reading backwards, in light of the resurrection, under the guidance of the Holy Spirit, can we understand both Israel's Scripture and Jesus' words."[38]

I concur, because we all stand on the shoulders of people like Hayes and others who have recognised that Scripture is best read in this way. In the preface, I referred to this practice as *reading backwards through a Holy Spirit inspired Christo-centric lens.* The churches I have pastored will affirm that I regularly speak of us reading backwards *through the eyes of Jesus.* The New Testament is in every way the Messianic interpretation of the Old Testament. Jesus, in the words of N. T. Wright, accomplishes everything that Israel could not accomplish.[39] Jesus is the fulfillment of every symbol, every type and every feast in the Old Testament. At the cry "it is finished" (*tetelestai*, τετελεσται) on the cross, the law, the prophets, the exile, the tabernacle, the temple, the priests, the sacrificial system, the rivers—literally of blood, the exodus, the kings, and the priests have all been fulfilled (*pleroo*, πλερω). When legalists quote Matthew 5:18 (NIV) to show that nothing will "disappear from the Law until everything is accomplished," the question deriving from that should be "well, when was all accomplished?" And the resounding cry comes from the cross: *it is finished.* At that point, the law is fulfilled and has done everything expected of it.

Jesus is the Messianic fulfillment of everything and every symbol in the Old Testament. When Jesus reads Isaiah 61 in the synagogue in Nazareth, he is proclaiming that the words are Messianically fulfilled in him. He does this early in his ministry as an announcement that in him the *Kingdom has come*—and *to introduce himself to the listeners as the long-time promised and awaited Messiah.* For all of us who follow him, his eyes are the eyes through which we read and understand the Old Testament. The early apostles wrote the gospels and the epistles, continuing in the tradition of Jesus, to give messianic meaning to the fulfilment of OT prophecy and in the events surrounding the birth, life, teaching, coming of the Kingdom, crucifixion, death, and resurrection of Jesus.

Everything we understand about Jesus, we understand after the events of his life. Everything we understand about the Old Testament we read through a Holy Spirit inspired, Christ-centred backwards reading, from the vantage point of the resurrection and the coming of the Holy Spirit. It pains me to see how some Christians, in a valid pursuit of discovering their Jewish roots, revert to a nearly Old Testament praxis that only vaguely resembles Jesus' messianic, New Testament interpretation of the Old Testament. Galatians 3:1, which says, "You foolish Galatians, who has bewitched you" does come to mind in the most radical expression of these reversions. We live in the New Covenant. *We are a people of the New Covenant.* The Old Covenant informs our understanding of the new and vice versa, but we are a New Covenant people. It is not possible to have one foot in the old and one in the new. By virtue of the nature of covenant, we cannot be in two covenants simultaneously. Yet so many believers practically are. We understand the Old Covenant and indeed the radical nature of the New Covenant by reading Scripture backwards through a Christological lens.

Scripture is a powerful tool, but like any tool, it can be used well and responsibly or it can be abused. Using Scripture is not about quoting verses or even about proof texting, as so many do. It is about seeing the main and the plain which is there to be found. Where the main and plain meaning of a text is not evident at a surface reading, it is about doing responsible hermeneutics and ***exegesis*** that determines the original context and meaning before attempting to apply it to our times.

> ***Exegesis*** uses all the linguistic and historical tools at our disposal in order to try and determine the original meaning of any text in its historical context.

CHAPTER 4

LIVING BETWEEN THE AGES: THE PROJECT OF NEW CREATION

"The resurrection completes the inauguration of God's kingdom...it is the decisive event demonstrating that God's kingdom really has been launched on earth as it is in heaven. The message of Easter is that God's new world has been unveiled in Jesus Christ and that you are now invited to belong to it."

N.T. WRIGHT

Eschatology is often thought of only in terms of searching for a linear timeline to the return of Jesus. The fuller meaning of the word, however, is to do with the study of final or ultimate things. The Greek word *eschaton* (εσχατον), which describes the ultimate destiny of creation and humanity, is likely more closely connected to another Greek word taken from philosophy, *telos*, than merely meaning the end of all things. *Telos* (τελος) refers to the goal, the ultimate purpose, or the intention and fulfillment of all things. The pursuit of a linear timeline to the return of Jesus is an exercise in futility. It is also in contradiction to any practically useful posture regarding working for the Kingdom now. After seeing a vision of the end and not understanding it, Daniel is urged by God *to go about his life until all things are revealed* (Dan 12:4). In the Vineyard people speak of the bride doing what the bride does until the bridegroom appears.

The promise of the Gospel is that one day there will indeed be a new heaven and a new earth. That heaven will, in the words of N. T. Wright, collide with earth.[40] And in this collision, there will be a restored and redeemed creation in which everything is the way that God intends for it to be and sin, sickness and death are vanquished. The New Testament speaks consistently of two ages: this age and the one to come. Old Testament prophets like Isaiah, Amos and others foretold of a future era when God would act decisively to intervene in human history to establish his rule and reign. Sometimes the two ages are used in the same sentence or verse. Sometimes only one of the ages is referred to.[41] On occasion the future age is referred to as a "new heaven and a new earth," other times as the "day of the Lord." But either way, it is always referring to a time when God will step into human history and establish his reign and rule in a way that eclipses anything that had preceded this day of the Lord.

In Luke 4:18 when Jesus reads from the Isaiah scroll, he is declaring that in him—Jesus—this day has come. In him, the age to come was beginning to break into the present age. But the arrival of Jesus the Messiah did not bring about the swift and immediate end to oppression, suffering and political turmoil that the Jews were hoping for. The Jews had of course read their own prophet Isaiah. Being under Roman oppression—and previously under other oppressors like Babylon and Assyria—they were expecting Messiah to come as *the conquering king* who would release them from the oppression of Rome by military victory (see Isa 59:21, 61:1–3, 61:10–62:12, 63:1–6). They failed to see the picture of Messiah in the same prophesy as *the suffering servant.* Jesus came as the suffering servant rather than as the conquering king the Jews were hoping for (Isa 50:4–9, 52:13–53:1).

> Jesus came to usher in the Kingdom of God as a present reality among us. It is a present reality that also points to a future reality where the Kingdom he has ushered in is ultimately consummated at his second coming. For now, we live in the time between the coming of the Kingdom and its consummation, with the presence of the future consummation evident in the present.

We live here, in these in-between times, *in the shadow of the cross.* Suffering, sin, sickness, and death are still with us and will continue to be with us until the "end of all things." But we have been authorised by Jesus to continue to usher in the things of his Kingdom until he comes (Luke 10:19). The Kingdom of God breaks in, as it did in Jesus, through healing, deliverance, salvation, care of the poor, advocacy, meekness, poverty of spirit, peacemaking, justice, and a multitude of other ways, giving us just a glimpse of what the fully consummated Kingdom will look like (Matt 5-7). In that way we are invited to be co-labourers, co-redeemers, and co-creators in the Kingdom with Christ (1 Co 3:9). To be busy being busy redeeming this world with him in every small or large act of kindness, care, goodness, advocacy, mercy, deliverance, salvation, provision, and indeed every good thing that is done in love. All of creation groans, says Romans 8:22, until the fulfillment of these things.

That profound theologian and philosopher, Gandalf the Grey, said it like this in the movie *The Hobbit*: "Some believe it is only great power that can hold evil in check. But that is not what I have found. I have found that it is the small every-day deeds of ordinary folk that keep the darkness at bay. Small acts of kindness and love."[42] We live between the ages in a Kingdom that is already here but not yet here in its fullness. Vineyard scholar Derek Morphew summarizes the times between the coming of the Kingdom and its consummation as being seen in four different biblical pictures of the Kingdom of God:

1. The Kingdom will come
2. The Kingdom has come
3. The Kingdom is coming immediately
4. The Kingdom will be delayed[43]

The present and the future Kingdom co-exist for a time until the end of the age. In Jesus, the presence of the Kingdom is seen in those he cured of diseases, his miracles, and those he healed of evil spirits. In the Church age, the presence of the Kingdom is seen in those things and many more. In John's Gospel, Jesus himself said that we (the Church) would do even greater things: "Very truly I tell you, whoever believes in me will do the works I have been doing, and they will do even greater things than these, because I am going to the Father" (John 14:12, NIV).

The New Testament records one quite lovely description of this in-between time that we live in. In 2 Peter 1:19, this time is described as the dawn. Dawn is an in-between time after the darkness of night is gone but the sun has not quite risen. Currently, darkness and light exist side by side. Both are present and both are absent. Neither is fully present and neither is fully absent.. Yet dawn holds a special promise. The promise is that the day will fully break. The night will pass, and the day will come. That is the hope we hold (Heb 10:23).

Nicky Gumbel tells a very simple story in the Alpha course to illustrate living between the times. He tells it to show how Jesus completely defeated Satan at his resurrection. When the Allies invaded Europe on D-Day and landed on the beaches at Normandy, on 6 June of 1944, WWII was effectively won. The German defeat was sealed on that day. Yet it took the Allies until May of 1945 to get that victory signed and sealed. It took them more than a year and 209,000 Allied deaths to consummate the victory that had been won nearly a year earlier. What happened between victory and consummation was an extremely costly mopping up operation.

KNOCKING ON HEAVEN'S DOOR: UNDER-REALISED ESCHATOLOGY

Under-realised eschatology tends toward defeatist faith. Whereas over-realised eschatology promises too much of the Kingdom now, under-realised eschatology promises too little! It does not really contain a significant vision for human flourishing in this world. Its expectation of God and the Kingdom in the here and now is severely hamstrung. At its worst it sees the Kingdom only as a future event, as something that is still coming on the other side of eternity. That begs the question then: *what did Jesus come to do?* The answer usually is that "Jesus came to die for my sin." As true as that statement is, it is at best partial. If all Jesus came to do was to die for my sin, then Herod should have got him when he was two years old (Matt 2:16). Jesus came to usher in the *presence* of the Kingdom with us now. The inheritance of the Kingdom is ours now, but it is not yet fully present. Jesus absolutely defeats sin, sickness, and death, and the consequence of that victory allows us to ask for *the presence of the future in the present.*[44]

> If all Jesus came to do was to die for my sin, then Herod should have got him when he was two years old.

If over-realised eschatology leads to inflated promises and claims, then under-realised eschatology hopes for little more than my salvation which I then cling to in the hopes of making it to heaven when I receive my inheritance. From this posture it becomes really challenging to live in the light of biblical injunctions to pray for one another's healing, for deliverance from spiritual and other maladies, or indeed for breakthrough of any kind. There is very little expectation (faith) for that. At its most extreme, under-realised eschatology leads to cessationism. In the pursuit of balance and orthodoxy, I have no intention of losing a legitimate desire and longing for the felt presence of God, nor to slide into the kind of defeatism that makes little impact for the sake of the Kingdom.

> The combined testimony of the Church through the ages is one of healings, deliverance from sin that held people captive, miraculous encounters with the Holy Spirit, and experiences that are at various levels inexplicable—yet attested to and promised throughout the pages of Scripture.

Many years ago, I was in a conversation with someone who asked me to pray with him for his healing from a life-threatening illness. I was surprised that he asked me this, because I knew he attended a high profile cessationist church in Cape Town. That church did not believe that God still did the things Jesus and the apostles did in the New Testament. He told me that the pastor of the church had visited him in hospital and left him with these words: "we all have our cross to carry." No prayer was offered, and no expectation from God in any way was evident. This despite the very simple biblical injunction in James 5:14 to call the elders to pray for you if you are ill. As an aside, outside of hermeneutical contortionism, I have no idea how cessationists explain away what amounts here to a very simple directive. I, and others, prayed with this man for his healing. In his case the physical healing did not come, and he later passed away from cancer. In other cases, I have seen healings that defy any scientific or medical logic. Not as many as I would have liked, to be sure. But enough for me to know that God does what God has always done. We are busy building *for* the Kingdom now and we do that with an expectation of the nearness and presence of God and with faith that eagerly expects heaven to regularly visit earth. Come Lord Jesus, come Holy Spirit!

"I'M A KING'S KID": TRIUMPHAL AND OVER-REALISED ESCHATOLOGY

Over-realised eschatology, on the other hand, all but ignores the suffering of the apostles that is so prevalent in the New Testament. It also tends toward having scant compassion for those who suffer now. It has no theology of suffering, despite the New Testament being replete with it.[45] Though the New Testament witness speaks consistently of trial, strife, enduring suffering patiently[46] and more, it quite literally avoids the shadow of the cross that falls on all believers and moves to a thoroughly cherry picked focus on the Kingdom being here now in all its fullness.

> At its worst, over-realised eschatology leads to triumphalism, the prosperity (health and wealth) gospel, and judgement on all who do not receive healing, or have wealth, or experience breakthrough. Advocates for this theology say that those who do not receive these things are lacking sufficient faith, or worse, hiding sin, and therefore cannot be recipients of these things. To the best of my knowledge, spiritual pride might well be the worst of all sins.

At its extreme, over-realised eschatology is graceless, lacks any compassion, and places an enormous burden of guilt and inadequacy on individual believers as praying incorrectly, lacking faith and just generally not measuring up to the super spiritual standards of those who apparently have these things. Its advocates leave other believers feeling inferior. Beyond the impact that this damaging teaching has on individuals, it often leads to the triumphal claims and desires for things like Christian Nationalist governance and dominionism. Christian Nationalism seeks power in a controlling hegemony. In that sense it is the over-realisation of the Kingdom without the cross. These desires are far more reminiscent of earthly power-based domination than they are of the upside-down power of the cross that is seen in its apparent powerlessness. Our authority, which is a translation of God's power in us, is seen in the posture that comes from the Sermon on the Mount and the fruit of the Spirit. It is meekness in the face of aggressive onslaught. It is peace-making between warring factions. It is mourning the state of our condition and creation. It is certainly not "victory through violence."[47]

INAUGURATED ESCHATOLOGY: ENGAGING THE NEW CREATION

Inaugurated eschatology recognises all four dynamics of the Kingdom: that it will come, it has come, it is coming immediately, and it has been delayed. These are somehow all at work simultaneously in the in-between time in which we live. The Kingdom we experience now is not just one of these things, it is the mysterious dynamic of all these things at play simultaneously. The Kingdom will come in its fulness when Jesus comes again to consummate his Kingdom. The Kingdom has already come in the incarnation of Jesus. The Kingdom is coming immediately any time we are building *for* the kingdom, whether in small acts of love or in great acts of salvation and deliverance by the Holy Spirit. The Kingdom has been delayed because Jesus (although continuously coming to us) will still come to us "on that day."

> When we can go about our lives with this as our posture, there will be a non-anxious presence about us. We will be those ambassadors of reconciliation that 2 Corinthians speaks of. We will be people who live with the expectation of the nearness, healing and presence of God, but without the misplaced zeal that lays a burden of expectation and guilt on those whom Jesus loves.

PRAYER RESPONSE

God the Holy Spirit, would you enable us *to live and to be* the people of your Kingdom from a place of deep settled trust in you, the Triune God. We recognise our propensity to move toward spaces that are not always good or healthy for us. We pray for the faith required to expect the nearness of heaven to be able to rearrange things on earth. We pray for the grace to be the people of the Sermon on the Mount even in the face of heaven not rearranging things on earth as we would have them.

CHAPTER 5

LEANING TOWARD JESUS: BELONGING IN A CENTRED SET

"True belonging only happens when we present our authentic, imperfect selves to the world. Our sense of belonging can never be greater than our level of self-acceptance."

BRENÉ BROWN

In Vineyard churches, the way that we choose to belong to our movement and to our local churches has always been central to our self-understanding. An important distinctive from most other neo-charismatics that emerged during our founding years is the Vineyard church's chosen model for belonging. We aim to belong in our communities as centred sets, rather than as fuzzy or bounded sets.

The centred set model for belonging was adopted by Vineyard from the work of the missiological anthropologist Paul Hiebert.[48] It defined our understanding of what it means to belong to a Vineyard church from the inception of the movement.

Bounded sets tend to have very tight defining boundaries regarding who belongs and who does not. In charismatic circles, bounded set belonging has often led to what is known as charismatic legalism. In a centred set the boundaries are far more fluid than in a bounded set. As long as the worshipper attending and participating at whatever level they choose to participate is moving towards the direction of the centre where we place Jesus, they are most welcome to be amongst us and to belong at the level that they choose to belong. Boundaries relating to morality, ethics, and scruples tend to be drawn at the level where people are being considered for a leadership role of some sort. The doors of Vineyard churches are open to all, but not all get to lead. This centred set way of belonging is a major departure from many other churches born of the neo-charismatic revivals. Many, if not most, have tended towards legalism and very tight boundaries of belonging.

BOUNDED SET BELONGING

In a bounded set, there are clear delineations regarding who is in and who is out. There is usually a precise and rigid path that determines how one gets into the closed inner circle of belonging. Such a path might stipulate things like completing a new member course or affirming a very detailed statement of faith and all accompanying doctrinal and other minutiae. There is a very clearly defined and rigid common centre with specific beliefs and rules relating to how to gather around the common centre. In charismatic circles this has sometimes led to unquestioning loyalty to a leader and to the church's stringent rules. Legalism, heavy shepherding, unquestioning loyalty, and non-accountability for the charismatic leader, and worse, tend to flourish in environments such as these.

> In charismatic circles, bounded set belonging has often led to what is known as charismatic legalism.

FUZZY SET BELONGING

Fuzzy sets are the opposite of bounded sets. They describe groups that have no organizational centre at all. Different parents who gather around their ten-year-old children's soccer or hockey team might well describe themselves as a group. There's a common interest, but there are no core values really that define or guide their existence as a group. This illustration describes a fuzzy set as a valid way of belonging, but only in very particular circumstances like the sports team illustrated. The Summer of Love of 1967 in Haight Ashbury, as a Hippie community, would have started as a fuzzy set, but the communes seldom ended up nearly as idealistically as the way they started out. Anarchism really doesn't work in community.

CENTRED SET BELONGING

In a centred set, the boundaries defining who belongs and who does not belong, and to what level they belong, are far more fluid than in a bounded set, but far more clearly defined than in a fuzzy set. There is a centre around which the group gathers. But the defining values of who belongs, and at what level they belong, has far more to do with *levels of involvement in the local Vineyard church*. The centred set way of belonging allows a worshipper to attend and participate at whatever level he or she chooses.

> Vineyard churches tend to trust that people are with us because they want to be with us, and that they are moving towards the centre, where we place Jesus. Vineyard does not ask diagnostic questions to determine someone's spiritual temperature for Jesus. People are welcome to be with us and to belong to us at the level that they choose.

Boundaries do tighten the more leadership falls to a person. In a very real way, this model of belonging has allowed Vineyard churches *to treat outsiders as insiders*, which has equipped us to welcome in the poor and the marginalized. Many have placed tight parameters around how to belong, and then been rigid regarding what one must do to fully belong to the group. Tighter boundaries make the task of pastoring easier for sure, but they favour the *rule of law over the Holy Spirit administering the church with us* as we listen for and submit to the Spirit's prompting continually. We are more inclined to err towards the ***antinomian*** edge, rather than erring toward the legalist edge. But that is because we are a New Covenant rather than an Old Covenant people. We live by grace, not by law. Come Holy Spirit!

Antinomianism **is the theological belief that rejects the authority of laws and moral norms. Vineyard most certainly does not reject the authority of laws and norms, rather we put them in their right place. We are a grace movement. We live under and by the continual prompting and guidance of the Holy Spirit.**

Vineyard has historically taken risks with people who others would scarcely allow through their doors, let alone give any leadership role. Vineyard churches do not have a register of church members nor a baptismal role that determines membership as it is understood in many denominations. So in our centred set way of belonging, the worshipper's voice is directly proportionate to his or her level of involvement in a particular local church.

Sometimes people ask me to illustrate this centred set way of belonging practically. I usually tell them the following story. I am a local church pastor. That means that Sunday in and Sunday out for about forty of the fifty-two weeks of each year, I not only go to the Sunday worship service, but I also preach or lead something there too. *There are Sundays on which I would rather be on the golf course.* On days like that, my direction is not leaning particularly intimately toward Jesus who is at the centre of all things. But he still loves me and does not reject me because I don't always feel like serving him. It might be that on such a Sunday, one or more of a group of substance-dependent street people come into the worship service from a place of *absolute desperation for Jesus.* They might have come, for the first time in their lives, to the very end of themselves and their deeply tragic existence. On such a Sunday, *these substance-dependent street folk are leaning closer into Jesus than I am.* They are, on such a day, way closer to the centre of who we are, and how we belong, than I am. Who am I to deny such people full belonging to the Church of Jesus Christ in every way they choose to belong? In any event, our whole culture is addicted to something. People living on the streets are merely symptomatic of us all. Our addictions, whatever they are, are no less indicative of brokenness than theirs. We are them and they are us.

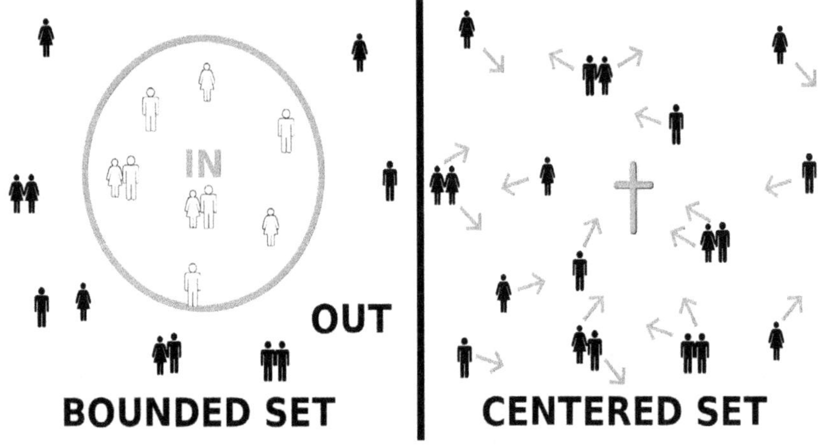

Figure taken from *Centered-Set Church: Community and Discipleship Without Judgmentalism* by Mark D. Baker.[49]

CHAPTER 6

"DO I BELONG HERE?"

"I dreamed about a culture of belonging. I still dream that dream. I contemplate what our lives would be like if we knew how to cultivate awareness, to live mindfully, peacefully; if we learned habits of being that would bring us closer together, that would help us build beloved community."

BELL HOOKS

A township in Canada refers to a subdivision of land that could be used for census purposes, or a municipal area. Townships are usually laid out in a grid system. In South Africa, the word township has a complex history that dates to the twentieth century with the **Native Land Act of 1913** and the **Group Areas Act of 1950** both contributing to racial segregation and the creation of African townships like *Soweto, Tembisa, Mamelodi, Alexandra, Mdantsane, Khayelitsha, Langa, Nyanga, Daveytown, Gugulethu, and Katlehong.* These townships, of which there are more than five hundred, are differentiated from informal settlements, of which there are thousands.[50]

The Natives Land Act, 1913 was aimed at regulating the acquisition of land. It largely prohibited the sale of land from whites to blacks and vice-versa. ***The Group Areas Act*** provided for the division of the country into areas based on racial categories determined by the government. This occurred during apartheid, when the white minority government implemented policies that sanctioned racial segregation and political and economic discrimination against the nonwhite majority.

As I explain this to Canadians, the usual response is "oh, so you mean a shanty town?" The answer would be yes, but also no. Most formal African townships in South Africa in 2025 are a mix of shanty town, formal housing that effectively becomes suburbia in the township setting, vibrant restaurant and ***shebeen*** life and more.

A ***shebeen*** was originally an illicit bar or club where alcoholic beverages were sold without a license. The term has spread far from its origins in Ireland, to Canada, the United States, the United Kingdom, Zimbabwe, the English-speaking Caribbean, Namibia, Malawi, and South Africa. In modern South Africa, many shebeens are now fully legal.

Entire communities, schools, libraries, police stations, hospitals, churches, mosques, subsistence farming, funeral homes, and more exist, live and function in the townships. There are dollar millionaires who choose the township life over and above moving to what is traditionally called "leafy suburbia." Soweto, outside of Johannesburg (Egoli), has a population of 1,271,628 according to the 2011 census. Khayelitsha, outside of Cape Town, has a population approaching 400,000 souls. Katlehong, in the municipality of Ekurhuleni, has close to a half a million inhabitants.

Under the same system of apartheid that created the ideological separation of people groups into places like townships, it was obligatory for all white men by the age of eighteen to be conscripted to military national service. Well, that is not entirely true. You had a choice. In 1980 when I was called up to military service, the choice was either two years of national service or six years behind bars as a conscientious objector. Or you could delay conscription by going to university or college straight after high school graduation. Studying first delayed the inevitable call up and gave you a better chance at receiving a commission during your national service years. Being a commissioned officer generally made life easier.

I chose to complete military service after high school graduation since I had no idea of what I wanted to study, if at all. I know people who chose the six years behind bars, but I was not, at seventeen years of age, yet mature enough to be convicted that this was something I possibly needed to consider ethically. So like most other young white boys my age, I served the mandatory two years of national service. I use the term boys intentionally—we were not yet men. I was seventeen when my call up came. After the two-year period, we were called back up to military camps each year for a total of nine months. These camps ranged from one to three months in duration and were disruptive to student and working life.

At the time I was conscripted, Apartheid South Africa was engaged in various military conflicts. The most noted was the so-called Border War.[51] It was a complex conflict that involved several nations including Namibia (then South West Africa), Angola, Cuba, and even the USA. I would be grateful even now if someone could explain to me what that was all about. It was South Africa's version of Vietnam. At that point of course, a handy epithet to apply to anyone seeking political independence from colonialism was communist. Communism did feature since many of the countries backing those fighting for liberation were Marxist, but the driving motivation to war was freedom from colonization.

My intention, however, is not to critique the rightness or wrongness of an extraordinarily complex, twenty-four-year-long and uniquely unpopular conflict. It is more important for me to tell a story that relates to my journey towards Jesus.

In my two years of national service, I served one border stint in which I was involved in Operation Protea[52] and found myself thirty kilometers into Angola with a brigade of junior leaders as a "practicum" of our training. Although we did see contact, which is a word used for military engagement, thankfully in both cases we had overwhelming fire power advantage and came out of those situations unscathed. The SWAPO insurgents, as they were called, were less fortunate.[53] After a nine-month officer's course that included the three-month border stint, I was commissioned as an Ensign (second Lieutenant) in 1 SA Marine Brigade. My second year of National Service consisted of protecting Durban harbour and oil refinery from potential so-called terrorist attack.

The most challenging assignment I saw during national service came a few months after completing the mandatory two-year service period. I was called up to do a one-month camp in a township outside of Johannesburg called Katlehong. At that time Katlehong housed resident migrant workers who worked in the mines. It was a political hotbed. The period during apartheid and just after apartheid ended was marked by extreme violence that included hostel attacks, assassinations, rape, and murder.

Many people who served stints in what was called *township duty*, along with those who lived in the township at the time, struggled with PTSD.

I have no intention of glorying in any exaggerated version of what I saw both in Angola and on a township tour. The best way to say it is that I would rather not have seen it. Our role was to patrol the township in sections of ten soldiers. Armed with military assault rifles and more, we were to keep the peace and then also to enter homes we felt might be a threat to that peace. That sometimes meant entering the homes of ordinary citizens and ripping them and their children out of bed at three o'clock in the morning. At twenty-one years old, the responsibility of commanding a platoon of three such sections weighed very heavily on me.

At that time, national servicemen were a hodge podge of differing political and humanitarian convictions, ranging from the rampantly racist to the begrudging participants in a system we had no control over. The task of commanding was fraught with pitfalls for me. *Controlling the rabidly racist* was always a challenge. Because of this mix of people, the Army, the Navy and the Air Force were far more popular in general in the townships than the South African Police Force (SAP). The SAP were ideologically more fully aligned with the whole apartheid ideology. This was because belonging to the SAP was always a chosen career rather than a forced conscription.

Thankfully, that dreadful month ended, and I was only called up to two additional, rather leisurely, one-month camps at naval bases after that. The second camp was as the officer on duty at the naval base SAS Unitie in Cape Town Harbour. Unitie was one of seven naval reserve bases. The reason I only did two additional camps was that as officer on duty, I had access to all the files that contained everyone assigned to that base's military record and history. In 1984, being the days before computerisation, I decided it was time to end my military career and destroyed my brown manila folder. I have never heard from the South African Defence Force again. I offered some mates of mine the same courtesy and for a promised night on the town, destroyed an additional five or so brown manila folders and their contents as well.

Although not yet a follower of Jesus at that point in my life, God had begun a work of ***prevenient grace*** and had brought me to a humanitarian awakening of a kind. The things I experienced during military service had wrought in me a *care and concern for the other.* I had come to the conviction that all humans are to be valued, all people matter. The ideology of apartheid was a grotesque caricature of the Christian faith, in what was held out as a Christian Nationalist vision. It took another few years to have my own profound conversion experience, which catapulted me into Jesus' Kingdom at twenty-seven years of age.

> ***Prevenient grace*** is a theological concept that refers to God's grace that prepares people to come to Jesus.

Fast forward to 2017. I am the Mission Centre Director (MCD) for South Africa of a Christian NPO based out of Colorado Springs, sometimes fondly called "Evangelical Springs." The NPO is Development Associates International (DAI) and it trains leaders for the Church in over seventy countries. My colleagues Sandra Naicker, Jele Manganyi, Babba Nicholas Wafula and I are headed for—you guessed it—Katlehong township, where we are going to make a plug to run workshops with a large group of Assemblies of God (AOG) leaders. *Of the more than five hundred formal townships spread across South Africa, this is the one to which we were called.* The AOG in South Africa, sadly, is the last of the major denominations I am aware of that is still split along racial lines.

Hard as that is to believe, it is unfortunately so. *Come Lord Jesus, come Holy Spirit!* Before running these workshops, our team needed to make a presentation to the senior leaders of the African branch of the AOG in South Africa.

Nicholas Wafula, a Ugandan then in his mid-seventies who headed up DAI East and Southern Africa, determines that I am the person to make the presentation. Most likely due to my vocal confidence and fast fading good looks. Jele is an AOG pastor himself and so feels it should not be him. Sandra, as a SAFFA with an East Indian background, is a little fearful of what her reception might be from a group of older African, mostly male leaders. So the presentation falls to me, mister vocal.

On arrival at the church where we were to meet, we are received and hosted with coffee, tea and treats in the usual hospitable African way. The group comprises the twenty most senior leaders in South Africa of the black AOG. I am encouraged to see some women among them. The time for the planned presentation of about twenty-five minutes comes and everyone is seated around a large conference table with yours truly taking the podium. The chairman prays for us and hands over to me. I open my mouth to speak, and…well, I literally cannot speak. The one who usually has things to say is rendered speechless. I start crying. I weep and weep and am struggling to stop. After about a minute of weeping, with my colleagues probably dying many quiet deaths, the AOG contingent, after what felt like an eternity of dead silence, gently start ***ululating***.

> *The Merriam Webster Dictionary* describes ***ululating*** as the uttering of a protracted rhythmical sound. An expression of joy, reverence, or sorrow.

Very quietly, in sung prayer, they offer their comfort by ululating for me, an erstwhile oppressor. A few minutes go by, and I regain my composure. I am offered a box of tissues and wipe the snot and tears away. As best I can, I offer something along the lines of, "I have been here before, but it was a very long time ago and I was carrying an assault rifle. Am I welcome among you?" The Chairman steps up to the mic and says words to this effect: "Let the past be in the past, our brother. You have been sent here by Jesus to help us lead his Church in a better way than we do it now. You belong with us. The floor is yours." The black arm of the AOG church in South Africa has become the mainstay of the work DAI now does in that country. I know that all of heaven celebrated on that day in 2017. Small is big in God's Kingdom.

> It took thirty-four years for me to discover that the bigger thing God was doing during my military National Service would come the full circle when I was fifty-four years old. The bigger thing was only witnessed by about twenty people on Earth. But it was also witnessed by that great heavenly host the writer to the Hebrews speaks of, a number too many to count.

CHAPTER 7

THE KINGDOM IN THE SHADOW OF THE CROSS

"Christianity teaches that, contra fatalism, suffering is overwhelming; contra Buddhism, suffering is real; contra karma, suffering is often unfair, but contra secularism, suffering is meaningful. There is a purpose to it, and if faced rightly, it can drive us like a nail deep into the love of God and into more stability and power than you can imagine."

TIM KELLER

Suffering, or even just difficulty or challenge, gives rise to the bigger universal principle of love. Love responds to these things. Love is peacemaking where there is conflict. Love can bring comfort when there is mourning. Love is meekness in the face of aggressive onslaught. In a very real way, we might not really know what love was, or what love is able to do, if not for the existence of suffering. Somehow in God's economy the bigger purpose of all suffering becomes then the response of love. *God is love.*

Freewill is a huge theological theme which cannot be discussed here outside of saying that I do not believe God ever violates the individual's freedom of choice, which he has bestowed on us (Gal 5:13).

My children have sometimes been frustrated with what they call my obsession with WWI and WWII. *Mea culpa…* "What's Dad up to? Oh, uhm, he's watching a documentary on the Battle of the Bulge." "Oh no! Freaking Hitler again!" These are some unsolicited glimpses into my family life. The reason I have this somewhat morbid obsession with war, or more specifically WWI and WWII, is that war illustrates the very best and the very worst of human nature. In the same trenches where one soldier is laying down his life for another, a different soldier is robbing the corpses of his own comrades for material gain. In the same debris of London after a Luftwaffe raid, some people are frantically digging for survivors and others are stealing jewelry from corpses. God has created us with a free will to choose good or bad. We have unlimited potential for good or bad in equal capacity, but history shows us that given the choice between good and evil our propensity is toward the latter—and I am no Calvinist.

Suffering somehow elicits a potential response that invokes love or evil in nearly equal proportion. The New Testament pages are filled with the reality and the theme of suffering. Not just ordinary human suffering or the human condition that we all endure, but more specifically, suffering for the sake of Jesus. That is suffering specifically for and because of what and whom we have been called to. And Christians are all called. As Os Guinness puts it, we are called "by God, to God and for God, everyone, everywhere, in everything."[54]

> The call to following Jesus has a significant cost attached. One of the terms of covenant is that my life is no longer my own (1 Cor 6:19-20). My life belongs to my covenant partner. Under the terms of the New Covenant, I belong to Jesus. My life is his to do with as he chooses. The New Covenant cost him everything, and it might cost me everything.

There are times when suffering for his sake will be part and parcel of what we are called to. Whilst we live in the reality of the coming of the Kingdom and however much God has for us in that, we are not ignorant nor dismissive of the existence of suffering, nor indeed the sometime call to it. If you think the term "call to suffering" is an exaggeration, then 1 Peter 2:21 is worth considering: "For to this you have been called, because Christ also suffered for you, leaving an example, so that you might follow in his steps" (ESV). The context of this passage is suffering for righteousness' sake, i.e., persecution for doing right in the face of unfair or even evil treatment. Like calling out sexually predatory behaviour in a church context and then facing ostracization, persecution, or condemnation for doing so. Or being a whistleblower in the corporate world when you discover fraudulent practice. Perhaps telling someone about Jesus in a secular space where you get hounded for sharing your faith. These things apply to all of us who live as citizens of the Kingdom in a world that does not know about nor want Jesus.

Years ago, when I was working in the corporate world in South Africa, I had a boss who drank way too much and who frequented strip clubs. I use alcohol, but I try to be careful around using it with people who have a drinking problem. I don't frequent strip clubs. I would always decline his invitations to a beer or a strip club. He had it in for me because he knew I would have a beer on occasion with other people. I will exclude the profanity, but he said to me, "no, you will not have a beer with me because you are way too self-righteous to have a beer with me." I really don't want to equate a small work-related challenge with the kind of suffering the New Testament writers speak of, nor with the suffering that believers in closed Muslim countries and other places now face for being followers of Jesus. But as society in the West becomes increasingly secularised, what is now a bit of a challenge and indicative of some marginalisation might in time become persecution. When I speak of persecution however, I am talking about the kind that could sometimes include the call to martyrdom. But all of us will *somewhere, sometime, be called upon to pay some kind of price* for following Jesus.

I find it exceedingly hard to write about the level of suffering I and my own family have faced because I know others who have paid a higher price. And then too I am aware of those who have paid the ultimate price. *I do not want to make out in any way that I am some kind of martyr. I am not. I am a follower of Jesus who, like most others, has known suffering.* My family and I have known suffering. Most of it just the ongoing, draining, bone wearying, and wearisome financial slog that so often comes with vocational ministry, when it really should not. (Can the Church of Jesus Christ please wake up!) The slow drip of never having enough to make headway and always needing to plug some financial hole or another, that is a reality for most who lay down their lives for the sake of the call. For my family, this resulted in the loss of one home due to financial pressure. But some of the suffering we have faced has been far more acute than financial struggle.

From the perspective of the watching and waiting world, televangelists and mega-church pastors flitting around in private jets could appear to be the normative situation in the Church of Jesus Christ. The reality is, however, that by far most people called to any form of vocational ministry—for want of a better word—struggle financially all their lives. In the years between 2002 and 2006 I accepted my first church call and ministered with the Anglican group referred to earlier, St. John's Parish Wynberg. I was called as the church planter and associate minister to St. Barnabas' Church in Kloof Nek Road, Cape Town. During the five years I spent as an Anglican ordinand, the bloody-mindedness of the ordination process combined with various broken promises and the fact that my family and I were made by the parish to move home four times in five years took an enormous toll. I ended up burned out in 2006 and spend most of 2006 and 2007 on medication. It was in these years we met the Vineyard and started cooperating with them.

When I hit rock bottom late in 2006, Vineyard was the natural place for us to flee to recover. Even now it is hard for me to think back to my time in the Anglican Church without significant pain. I am telling these stories not to wallow nor to lay blame, but to illustrate that our reality is very normative for people in church ministry. I accept whatever blame was mine in these situations. Very few of my friends and colleagues in ministry have not suffered at least somewhat for the sake of the call.

Sometimes my own family has suffered for decisions I made believing that I had heard Jesus quite clearly before making them. These decisions were not necessarily universally appreciated by colleagues and other followers of Jesus. Between 2014 and end 2016 I faced three years of significant persecution after laying down the call to a local church I had pastored. The attempts to discredit me included a former colleague trying to block me from employment at a time when we were going through torrid financial strife. Those years were terrible. The detail is irrelevant; it is sufficient to say they were for my family the years from hell. And here is the challenging thing: it was other believers, some we had loved and cared for significantly, who were instrumental in our persecution. It was biblical in proportion. Sometime during those three years I hit a very dark place and was unsure that I would ever pastor a local church again. As a person whose nature is usually fairly sunny and optimistic, I became quite melancholy for extended periods and had a season of depression. Somewhere during that season, I wrote one of only two attempts at poetry. It's likely *not the greatest poem* you will ever read, but it captured my mood very well. My second poem, which you do not get to see, is way better although also quite bleak. It does seem I am only driven to the poetic in times of struggle.

The weariness of long-lived sorrow
diminishes hope held tomorrow
yet, to know beyond the pain
we live to see the greater gain.
Not only when we stand in glory
but within this temporal story.
Though all our dreams in tatters lie
Kingdom comes from God on high.
The day will dawn when it breaks through
and God will do what God will do.
Upon that day, when he restores
the King will win our long liv'd wars
and we will be redeemed and lifted
sorrow, pain, and strife is shifted.

We had only just begun to emerge from this horrific season and had managed to buy a home again, when disaster struck a second time. It was as if we had just come up for breath, when in January 2019, a raging fire took our home in Betty's Bay[55] along with our dog and everything we owned. *And very real suffering was our reality.*

As you read this you may reasonably ask, "well how was losing your home suffering for the sake of Jesus? Was that not just ordinary human suffering, the kind that every person is liable to face somewhere and somehow?" I would answer yes, and also no. Yes, because forty other homes in Betty's Bay were taken in the same fire and all those people suffered loss through fire too. No, because God spoke in the fire. And what he spoke was a reaffirmation of *the cost of the call.* The day after the fire Caleb Pederson,[56] a friend and Vineyard colleague and mentee who also owns property in the area that was ravaged by the fire, was wandering around on our smoke-filled lot of land. In his walking about he came upon a scrap of paper, the only surviving scrap from a library of theology of about 1,000 books. Here is the scrap of paper. I leave it for you to decide what God might have been saying to us.

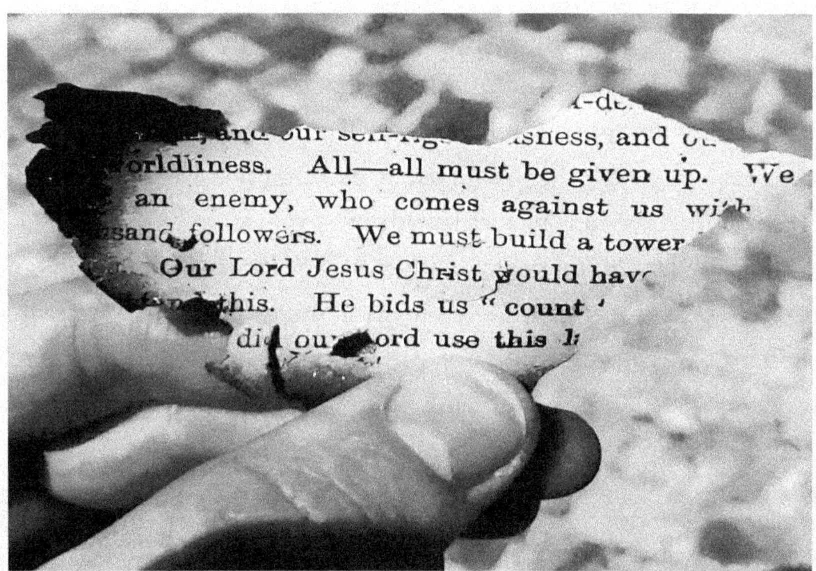

We have not been able to buy property again, but live in the hope that we ultimately will, and are trying to save toward the same. My family has known suffering and has known it specifically because our lives are entwined with Jesus.

Our children have on occasion asked me why it seems that our family has suffered more than most other people that they know. Sometimes they have said to us "maybe life would be easier for us if we were not Christians." The reality is that somehow, mysteriously, as followers of Jesus, our lives are bound up in the suffering of our Saviour. We will share in his sufferings. It is a privilege we will likely only appreciate when the Kingdom fully comes on his return, or when we are called home.

In January of 2025, as I write, my wife Anida and I are living with Christian friends in Langley, British Columbia until we settle fully into the lower mainland of the province later this year. These friends are a lovely, kind, hospitable, funny, quirky, and generous couple the same age as us. They have kindly offered us hospitality until we settle more permanently. We occupy the ground floor of their home. They have most of the things that people long for to make us feel secure: a magnificent home on a large acreage in Langley, a beautiful and large family, their health, and no obvious material need. Just over two years ago, they lost an adult son in a motor vehicle accident. They know suffering of a kind I do not even want to think about. Is it the kind of suffering that is common to all of humanity? Yes, it is. But somehow, knowing them, I suspect it is also linked to sharing in the sufferings of Christ. I cannot begin to imagine their pain and loss.

Sometimes we see suffering visited on whole communities or even countries. When proponents of the so-called prosperity gospel, *which is no Gospel at all*, come into poverty-stricken communities of deeply devout followers of Jesus in Africa, Asia or South America, and berate and belittle them for their lack of faith, may the Lord himself have mercy on them. When we have done such disgraceful things in the name of Jesus, then we have in every conceivable way broken the third commandment not to take the Lord's name in vain. There is something about visiting poor communities who follow Jesus with their whole heart in places in Africa which makes you realize that you are *standing on holy ground.* Be very careful of dismissing the call and indeed, at times, the gift of suffering. God is busy with way bigger things than you or I can see. This is not a fictitious illustration. I am aware of several real-life situations in which this misplaced and rather obscene judgment has been visited upon individuals and whole communities.

> The reality is that somehow, mysteriously, as followers of Jesus, our lives are bound up in the suffering of our Saviour. We will share in his sufferings.

Our lives in the kingdom that is available to us now are lived *in the shadow of the cross.* The cross and the Kingdom go together, which is why Christians are to serve rather than to dominate. We are sometimes much like the Apostle Peter when he rebukes Jesus for suggesting the suffering that lay ahead for him, "God forbid it Lord, no such thing will ever happen to you!" Jesus' response to Peter and to you and me is simply that:

> *Whoever wants to be my disciple must deny themselves and take up their cross and follow me. For whoever wants to save their life will lose it, but whoever loses their life for me will find it. (Matt 16:24-25, NIV)*

Poor old Pete. *Shimon*—Simon—Peter who is still on his way from being a "reed" (Simon) to becoming a "rock" (Peter). He doesn't get it. He only wants the victory of our faith. The good stuff. He does not understand what it is that he has signed up for. Nor do we.

> We will walk with Jesus, the road to Calvary, before we experience the glory of the resurrection.

In Dietrich Bonhoeffer's words, "when Christ calls a man, he bids him 'come and die.'"[57] Abandonment to the one we are wed to. We are wed to only one. His name is Jesus, and his sufferings are ours.

CHAPTER 8

"WOULD THAT HAVE HAPPENED?"

"A man's daughter is his heart."

MAT JOHNSON

Following our hellish season, which I have already referred to as the years from 2014 to end 2016, we "holed up" in our home in Betty's Bay in 2017. We were slowly recovering, rebuilding, and re-emerging. That was the same home that was taken by the fire in January of 2019. I really doubted that I would ever pastor a local church again. When the Vineyard church in Yellowknife, in the Northwest Territories of Canada, extended the call to us in 2018, they were unaware that we had been in a season away from any local church. We had been churchless for four years. My family, my red rocker and my mountain bike and back-pack with a Bible in it had been my church.

There was a day when I had cycled out into the mountains for about twenty kilometers and decided to take a time out to read, pray and reflect. It was a time when most of my devotions were prefaced by the cry "why Lord?" On that morning, seated in the ***fynbos*** with my Bible in hand, I cried to the Lord again, "why Lord? Why did you tell me to let the church go and to lay down the call? We were on an upward trajectory and had grown from around one hundred and fifty people upon our arrival to what was a deeply troubled church, to approaching three hundred souls. We were a solid family-sized church on an upward trajectory toward becoming a large, ethnically diverse church by South African Vineyard metrics. Why Lord?" I heard the Spirit as clear as a bell on that morning: *"To prevent you from becoming all the arrogant things that you react against, Melt."* I stopped asking God why around about then.

Fynbos **is a small belt of natural shrubland, or heathland vegetation, located in the Western and Eastern Cape of South Africa. The area is predominantly coastal and mountainous.**

Our kids and friends regularly came to our home a hundred kilometers up the East Coast from Cape Town. One Friday morning in early 2017, we received a call from our eldest daughter Marie' to say that she and her sister Simone were coming up for the weekend from Cape Town. Clearly the two of them had been scheming. Simone had followed Jesus most of her life, from the time that she was a small girl. Marie' had taken somewhat of a detour in her teens and was more affected by being a pastor's kid, it seemed. In 2014, she had come to a spiritual awakening and had stepped back into her faith with the energy and commitment that comes only from renewal by the Holy Spirit. Both Marie' and Simone were attending Woodstock Community Church, a small Vineyard church in Cape Town. That church now goes by the name of Signal Vineyard and is likely the fastest growing Vineyard church in South Africa.

The two colluders had decided it was time for them to come and minister to the folks. They railroaded us. We were completely unaware of any agenda beyond a usual weekend visit. Their younger sister Emma had once landed in some trouble at school for writing a composition in which she had said that *her two older sisters flew to school on their brooms* every morning. The witches had clearly been colluding in this instance again. To our ~~detriment~~ benefit. Somewhere on that weekend they sat us down on the sofa and started to pray for us. All heaven broke loose. I was lying on the floor bawling and Anida my wife was howling with laughter, despite her not being in that frame of mind. Usually, those things would have been the other way around, but the Holy Spirit knew what he was doing. Our daughters were praying for us and also prophesying to us. I do not remember too many specifics and Anida remembers even less. But I do remember one of them prophesying rather non-liturgical words over me that ran something like this: *'And as for you, old man, if you do not get back into pastoral ministry, you are going to die a sad old git.'*

All eventually settled down and Anida and I started talking and praying over the next few weeks about what this all might mean. A month or so later we determined that God was calling us back into pastoral ministry, but not in South Africa. We began the search. I asked her "where?" She said, "maybe the UK or Europe. Not the USA." I said, "what about Canada, all the best Vineyard musos are there." Anida replied, "hmmm, very cold." I googled "Vineyard churches in Canada seeking lead pastor." At the time, the only Canadian Vineyard looking for a pastor was Yellowknife Vineyard Church. It popped up. I was sitting at the desk in my office, and Anida was in the kitchen. My office was an open plan office upstairs, overlooking the kitchen downstairs. Anida was in her happy place cooking up a storm. I said something like, "oh, here's an interesting one, Yellowknife…looks like it's quite far north." Anida says, *'how far north?'* I go, "uhm let's see, uhm, '420 kilometers south of the Arctic' kinda north." Anida says, "After everything we have been through, I am seriously not living in the freaking Arctic, Melt!" I reply, "It's not in the Arctic, it's 420 kilometers south of the Arctic." The rest, as they say, is history.

The interesting part of what unfolded is that ultimately it was Anida who received the confirmation that we would go to Yellowknife. That happened on a day when the call committee who was interviewing us told me to go away so that they could speak to Anida. They spoke to her for over an hour. After that conversation she came to me and said, "we are going to Yellowknife." It was the first time in eighteen years of ministry in and around the Church, in two different church groups, that any leader had been vaguely interested in her or shown any real concern for her. In the past any call I had received had involved conversation with me only. Anida came along for the journey. Her opinions or sentiments regarding the call, or anything else for that matter, were never solicited, requested or required. That day, a small Vineyard church in the Northwest Territories of Canada heard her, affirmed her and in so many ways set her free.

In a process of six months leading up to our first visit "with a view to a call" to Yellowknife, we sought the Lord and heard certain things clearly. One of the things I heard was that this call was more about Anida than it was about me. This certainly proved to be the case. Anida is a chef and has her own career and passions. She loves Jesus and has an extraordinary God-given capacity for deep and authentic friendship—way bigger than mine—but has never felt called to ministry per se. She has been an incredible and faithful support to me always, but as she says, she "does not do meetings or play the piano" or carry the identity of being a pastor or even a pastor's wife. Yet at Yellowknife Vineyard Church she became all the things that past dismissal had always made her extremely wary of. She became a beloved figure in the church. I watched her for six years as she went about doing all the things that had previously frightened her. Really all because someone, somewhere made her feel heard and cared for. On our journey of relocating to Yellowknife, God showed me things I needed to know to accept the call to a different and distant country. Some of those things have come to pass here in Canada, some I hold to with hope.

On our visit to Yellowknife in June 2018, "with a view to a call," we were received and hosted by Vineyard leaders in Edmonton en route to Yellowknife. Of particular note is a lunch that we had in Ruth Rousu's home along with her son and daughter-in-law Nathan and Charis, Terri Harsch, and Carol Lovejoy. After lunch, the team were praying us on our way, and Carol emerged from the kitchen. She basically read our mail. It was quite profound. She was given insight into our lives and glimpses of our present and future. We flew to Yellowknife knowing that we would be relocating to Canada. After two weeks in Canada, we flew back to South Africa and began the process of getting our paperwork and visas in line with Canadian immigration requirements.

While we were back in South Africa, I was having a conversation with our eldest Marie' when she said, "Dad, you remember when we came to pray for you and Mom eighteen months ago at Betty's?" I responded, "well how could I forget love?" She said, "do you think that would ever have happened if Kenilworth had grown to a thousand people and you were still the senior pastor there?" I said, "probably not." Bigger things. Just way bigger things than you and I can begin to imagine. By human metrics, not that impressive really. In God's economy the acceptance and embracing of Anida, the privilege of having our adult children praying for us and setting us free to do what God was calling us to do? Those things might just be way bigger than being the pastor of a thousand strong church. Small is big in God's Kingdom.

We relocated to "Yellowsnake," as one of our South African friends misnamed it, in November of 2018. At that time Yellowknife Vineyard Church was a small community of just over one hundred people in a city of 20,000.

CHAPTER 9

PLATO AND THE GNOSTIC JET STREAM

"Who needs an external God? No one in the church of the serpent does. Two can play the expulsion game. If God expels us from his Eden, we can expel him from our Eden, because only we ourselves are now gods. The Olympian gods replaced the older generation of gods, the Titans. The old gods are always replaced. The biblical God too must be replaced."

DAVID SINCLAIR

Gnosticism is a term that describes a diverse, ***syncretistic*** spiritual movement that flourished from the second to the fifth centuries AD in the Mediterranean region. The word comes from the Greek word *gnosis* (γνωσις) meaning knowledge or insight. My own conviction is that it originated in the first century AD and was already entrenched and flourishing in places like Ephesus by the time John penned his Gospel, some decades after the Synoptic Gospels of Matthew, Mark, and Luke.

Syncretism **is the process of combining different ideas, beliefs, and practices together to create a new whole, or belief system.**

Most of us who were taught about Gnosticism at seminary in the 1980s or 90s thought it a rather quaint and irrelevant belief system until Dan Browne's bestseller *The Da Vinci Code* catapulted Gnosticism into full view again. In 2003 when the book was published, I was asked to do a talk on it and host a Q&A session for St. John's Parish in Wynberg Cape Town, held at Christ Church in Kenilworth. The Christian—more specifically Roman Catholic—world was in a bit of a quandary around what was, by Browne's own acknowledgement, essentially a fictitious novel. In my talk I did refer to the book, but I tailored it more around Gnosticism in general than *The Da Vinci Code* specifically. At about the same time there was significant noise around the writings of Elaine Pagels and others regarding the discovery of the Gnostic gospels such as the gospel of Thomas. These gospels were in fact discovered way earlier, and we have been well-aware of their existence since their discovery at ***Nag-Hamadi*** in Egypt in 1945. Christian scholars have been studying them for decades and there is absolutely no conspiracy to keep them out of the mainstream, as some would have it.

The ***Nag Hammadi*** Library (also known as the Chenoboskion Manuscripts and the Gnostic Gospels) is a collection of early Christian and Gnostic texts discovered near the Upper Egyptian town of Nag Hammadi in 1945.

These Gnostic gospels are very different from the Gospels of Matthew, Mark, Luke, and John. The canonical Gospels tell this very Jewish story that shows how Jesus announces a different Kingdom from the kingdom of Caesar. Jesus' announcement shows how God is becoming King on earth just as he is in heaven. The Gnostic gospels read very differently. Their Jesus is teaching and dispatching *esoteric wisdom sayings* through which people can gain a different perspective on their lives and discover a "divine spark" within. The Gnostic Jesus tends to represent the New Age fare on which our culture feeds and has a very weak claim, if any, to representing the historical Jesus. The Gnostic gospels are valuable to us however, since they help us to contextualise the Ancient Near East and the culture in which the Early Church ministered.

A list of additional resources for further reading is provided at the end of *Bigger Things*. For now, it is sufficient to reassure the reader that the canonical Gospels of Matthew, Mark, Luke, and John *have every single authentic reason to claim to go back to the life of the historical Jesus himself* rather than for example the gospels of Thomas or of the Egyptians, which really have no historical claim whatsoever to authentically portraying the life of Jesus. The canonical Gospels are about the God who says "I am reclaiming this world because it is my good creation. It is my lovely, beautiful creation, and you humans are a wonderful piece of that creation. You are, in fact, the high point of that creation, because you are made in my image and are now going to be reborn to discover and to usher in the redemption of everything."

> The canonical Gospels tell this very Jewish story that shows how Jesus announces a different Kingdom from the kingdom of Caesar. Jesus' announcement shows how God is becoming King on earth just as he is in heaven.

A quote taken from my doctoral project explains why I believe Gnosticism might have emerged even earlier than traditional teaching says:

> These arguments would be difficult to sustain outside of recognising that Gnostic teaching was a real challenge to the early church. It seems likely that the onset of Gnosticism ran almost concurrent with the emergence of the orthodox Christian faith. I.e., Gnosticism likely emerged even earlier than has traditionally been taught. This is from my perspective, at least one of the reasons why John's Gospel is so very different from the Synoptics. By the time John penned his Gospel, (dating ranges from AD 70 to AD 110 in its final form) Gnosticism was an existing problem he was addressing. The Synoptics penned a few decades earlier did not see the need to engage the issue to the extent that John appears to address it. It is not impossible that John's Gospel is written with situations like those being addressed in Ephesus in mind. There is no doubt that Gnosticism had already begun to influence the Christians at Ephesus. Women in the congregation, being given practically no education at that time, were far more

> likely to be led astray by Gnostic teaching and beliefs than the men in the congregation. Contrary to Bultmann and the school of dialectical theologians, who argued that John's Gospel contained elements of Gnosticism, I would argue that John's use of language and concepts already known to first century Greeks and Gnostics are clear examples of doing contextual theology. When John says for e.g., that the "Logos became flesh" he is indeed saying something beyond what was dreamt of by Philo, or the other Greek philosophers. But in every other respect it is their Logos. John's Logos is the cosmic Mediator between God and the world, who is the personification of God's truth and wisdom. John takes this further when he asserts that Christ is in fact the Logos' incarnation and fulfilment. The point is that John uses a term already known to Jews and Greeks and the Gnostics within and fully reveals Christ to them by using that familiar term. The same applies to his continuous use of "light versus darkness" and other similar themes used throughout the Gospel and the body of Johannine literature. He is speaking the language already known to the Gnostics, in order to introduce the Christ to them.[58]

Describing Gnosticism is not an easy task. It came, and still comes, in many forms. Essentially though, the Gnostic is one who claims to have secret knowledge over and above what traditional wisdom, science, philosophy, theology and education have as ***epistemology***. Of course, since the advent of the internet and social media, we are surrounded by "those who really know" about pretty much every topic. The decade ahead might be about discerning where we get our news from as much as anything else. Accepting that when it comes to the political sphere any objective reporting has *likely never existed*, there are spaces I tend to go to over and above other spaces. Each of us will have to discern those things for ourselves moving ahead and I have no intention of promoting Reuters over the BBC or whomever else. I will however say just this as cautionary. Whoever still believes that the alternative independent newsfeeds all over the internet have no bias or agenda like CNN or CBC indubitably do have, needs to have their minds read. The only certainty I currently have about many of the alternatives is that they might be the only thing generally worse than the mainstream media!

> ***Epistemology*** **is the theory or study of knowledge. It is a branch of philosophy that examines how people come to know things and the limits placed on such knowledge.**

That as an aside. But not entirely an aside, because Gnostic thinking feeds into and out of this as our current context. N. T. Wright speaks of Gnosticism as being the default religion of the USA for over two hundred years.

> Early Gnosticism taught that our physical bodies were temporary, unsatisfactory and despicable in every way—evil even—and were at best a box that housed the real part of a person, the spirit. The idea was that our spirit would escape this dreadful home that it was trapped in. Gnosticism is dualistic and in a very real way rejects the created order.

The Early Church, in contrast to that idea, always taught two things:

1. The created order is good (Gen 1:31), and is to be redeemed, not rejected. That includes our bodies which will ultimately be redeemed and raised to new life.
2. That our hearts are deceitful above all things and our inner identity is something Jesus can heal and redefine for us. *No secret knowledge is required. The Gospel is at its root quite simple.*

Let's take a deeper dive into ancient Gnosticism and then consider where and how it has affected the Church today, most notably in the North Americas. Vineyard scholar Derek Morphew published a study of ancient and contemporary Gnosticism in April 2000.[59] Of all that Derek has written, it is this piece which I have returned to time and again. I have referred people to it regularly, and I have read way broader on the subject myself since I first became aware of it in the mid 1990s. *The Spiritual Spider Web* is still as relevant as when Derek penned it.

David Brakke wrote an extremely helpful book for those who want to read deeper into the Gnostic belief system.[60] He covers in depth the various Gnostic communities that existed between the first and fourth centuries AD, their similarities, overlaps, departure points and so on. These communities were very diverse, but the common thread is the desire for *gnosis* (knowledge). All these groups were rejected by what eventually became orthodox Roman Catholic Christianity. They were all regarded as heretics. Orthodox Christianity became what it is today, in part, in response to these teachings of *gnosis*. The consistent themes which can be seen throughout are:

- Advanced knowledge ("we know stuff that you don't know")
- Myth making
- Mystical union with the divine

- Material universe as seriously flawed and bad; in extreme cases, not even something God intended
- As a result, earth is not our true home, we need to escape it
- As a result, the god who created this mess cannot be the highest god
- We know the true God

Prior to the 1945 discoveries at Nag Hammadi, most of what we knew about Gnosticism came from Irenaeus of Lyons. He was a Greek bishop who lived in Lyons, Gaul (France). He lived from about 120 to 203 AD. He wrote *Against Heresies* in 180 AD. Irenaeus was not the most objective voice from which to learn about Gnosticism since he regarded the group as completely apostate and so was scathing in his critique. The Nag Hammadi discoveries have given us a better perspective on the very intricate belief systems of these various Gnostic communities that included Valentinianism, Sethianism, Docetism, Manichaeism, Mandaeism and more.

I believe that the repeated problems the Epistle writers faced and addressed across the pages of the New Testament could be summarised as just two things: *Gnosticism and legalism.* And, as we shall see, the two are not mutually exclusive. Morphew writes, "Gnosticism arose into the confused world into which the gospel was [first] proclaimed. It was a time when the older religions were losing ground and new ones were gaining popularity."[61]

To separate Gnosticism from the Gospel which the New Testament writers were proclaiming, we must visit some philosophical assumptions. The Gospel writers wrote from the assumption that truth was an objective reality, and that God was revealing himself in the redemptive history of his people in mighty acts, and indeed on the pages of the Old

Testament. Ultimately that approach toward Scripture was observable once the New Testament canon too was concluded. Essentially, we could call that approach the study of God's observable acts in history. Our confessions of the faith, such as the creeds, all proclaim that there is an objective revelation of God through the ages that we can track in the canon of Scripture and in the collective witness of the Church. Theologically, we call it the meta-narrative, or overarching story, of God in creation and history.

Gnosticism's approach to any truth claim was based in something entirely different. Gnosticism, being in essence ***dualist*** and mystical, bases its truth claims *in the mystery of the experiential.* Because as Christians we have our own experiential dynamic at play,[62] we are more open than most to moving into what I have called *the gnostic jet-stream.* The challenge is that during times of renewal when people are having all sorts of experiences in the Spirit, things can go whacked. "Whacked" is a theological term I have coined and am asking for its inclusion in the Oxford Dictionary of theology. At this point, unless we are grounded in the more objective things of our faith—the simple and ancient paths that keep us anchored—we can move into this gnostic jet stream wherein all valid reality becomes experiential only.

> ***Dualism*** is the philosophical idea that reality is made up of two fundamental types of things. These things are usually diametrically juxtaposed. They are posited as extreme opposites rather than integrated wholes. Spirit and body or spirit and physical matter would be the two types of things Gnostics would juxtapose.

Further chapters offer what I believe is necessary and available to keep us open to the experiential without losing our grounding. This includes Scripture reading, the creeds, the ancient spiritual disciplines and indeed, weighing the experiential in community. The reality is that mystical and Spirit given experience *never* matches or mirrors reality in a logical and sequential way. Being one who is very grateful to have had mystical experiences in the Spirit over thirty-five years, I know this practically. I also know it from reading the **Apocalyptic** books in Scripture.

> ***Apocalyptic,*** from the Greek ***apokalupto*** **(αποκαλυπτω).** This form of literature has to do with prophesying and describing the imminent end of all things. It uses significant imagery and metaphor to illustrate a momentous struggle and battles. It means "to reveal, or to uncover" something mysterious.

When cessationists and dispensationalists interpret Scriptures like Ezekiel and Revelation, it is apparent that they have no idea what to do with them. Being intrinsically opposed to any possibility of experience in the Spirit themselves, they interpret those books through the logical and linear lenses they know. Apocalyptic literature just does not function in that way at all. At the other extreme, we are now faced with followers of Jesus who have by all indications discarded the ancient paths and practices that have always kept us in orthodoxy.[63] The story that follows is a practical illustration of how the Church, devoid of tried and tested spiritual practices, can move collectively into an entirely Gnostic approach to the experiential.

At the turn of the twenty-first century, I visited a local church in Cape Town in a suburb called Durbanville, where my family lived at the time.

Someone in the church had had a vision that had been shared with the pastor. The pastor decided that this vision needed to be shared with the church. Nothing too strange or untoward so far. I happened to be visiting on the Sunday that the vision was shared. The words of the vision were typed up onto what was in those days an OHP and projected onto a screen. Each sentence was numbered as we would number, say Genesis 1:1-13. So, it was for practical purposes, "Leroy 1:1-57" (dear old Leroy). The pastor then exegeted the vision verse by verse, exactly as any preacher would teach an expository sermon. No invitation to weigh the vision was offered. It was held out as any Old Testament prophet would hold it out in a "thus says the Lord" fashion. We are faced with four problems I can recognise in this way of viewing the experiential:

1. It elevated the experiential to canonical status and more. In that sense, it was supra-scriptural. Some readers might say that *Bigger Things'* plea for going beyond Scripture to land in a good interpretation of Scripture is also supra-scriptural, and they would be correct. However, when scholars move beyond Scripture to interpret it well, they do so in a biblically informed way.
2. It allocated way too strong an objective truth claim, in the inevitable subjection that is personal *experience*.
3. It invited no communal weighing or discernment.
4. It did away with the need of going to Scripture at all—not that every worship service needs to go to Scripture in every situation. But it did illustrate a certain general posture toward the Scriptures.

Let's expand a bit more on Gnosticism and neo-Platonic thought before offering any corrective. Scholarly consensus recognises that Gnosticism likely first infiltrated Hebraic thought during the exile to Babylon. The Persians held to a dualism of light (good) and darkness (evil) that were seen to be equally powerful opposites. The Hebrew exile to Babylon was in the sixth century BC. About two hundred years later, the Greek philosopher Plato taught a dualism between the ideal and the material world: he separated those two things as irreconcilable. In his teaching, the material world stands as antithetically opposed to the spiritual world and all material reality is regarded as inherently evil. This teaching stands in stark contrast to the Judeo-Christian teaching that all material reality was *created good by God* but has fallen.

Gnostic tendency is sometimes seen in the Church when followers of Jesus dismiss the material in favour of the so-called spiritual. In that thinking for example, a prayer meeting might be seen as far more important to Jesus than a chat over a cup of coffee with someone who really needs an ear. Or an intercessory group becomes by default the spiritual gurus in a church, when in fact prayer belongs to everyone. It is not difficult to see how attractive portions of Gnostic and neo-Platonic thinking can be to charismatic Christians. We are rightfully attracted to spiritual things because God has created us ***Imago Dei*** as spiritual, physical, emotional and psychological beings (1 Cor 12:31). The desire for spirituality is a legitimate and God-given desire. It only becomes skewed when the *so-called spiritual* is elevated over the so-called ordinary or mundane. In one way, our whole language of spiritual formation, if adopted uncritically or in an unthinking way, can become problematic. Leonard Sweet observes that "The whole language of the 'spiritual life' is part of our problem. There is no spiritual life. There is only life. One life where the spiritual is not separate but the whole."[64]

Imago Dei is a Latin phrase meaning in the image of God. It conveys that we share in the nature of God and are meant to reflect his dignity and character on earth. Practically it means that we are unique beings in creation, sharing qualities such as rational thinking and the ability (beyond mere instinct) to love and care for others.

Evidence of Gnosticism is also seen in the contemporary Church when followers of Jesus elevate evil to proportions that are not what Scripture teaches about it. Satan is a created being who exists until such time as the Kingdom comes in its fulness.

Scripture says Satan will be cast into something called the abyss. He does not now, nor has he ever, had the kind of power that some Christians ascribe to him as though he sits just below God and not as part of the created order. This not to discount the reality of Satan's existence nor his incredibly high work ethic! That might be the only commendable thing about him—he works really hard. The saying "works like the Devil" is accurate enough.

Gnostic thinking is most noticeably seen in the sometime extremes of charismatic believers who become "super spiritual." The ones who always seem to have secret knowledge that mere mortals and ordinary disciples of Jesus like you and me don't have. A dismissive smile in a space in which you have been asked to teach that tells you the smiler has secret knowledge that you are not privy to. Paul refers to these people as "super-apostles" (2 Cor 11:5). Those who are prophetically called and gifted must always be on guard against adopting the spirit of super apostolicity.

Gnostic tendencies are also seen in the all too prevalent thinking that says that we live in the most evil of all ages. Really? Honestly? Whilst evil is insidious and is always at work in every age, including our own, there are incredible progresses that have been made in the basic humanity-affirming practices that Christian influences have brought to the world. Wright and Bird point out:

> For all the evils of Christendom, with its marriage of Church and State, with the duumvirate of bishop and king, there were *genuinely positive, and ultimately revolutionary changes for human civilization.* Political liberalism, far from being the formidable foe of Christianity, proves in fact to be its lost child, who refuses to believe the truth about its paternity (John 3:16).[65]

Aside from political liberalism being the lost offspring of the result of Christian influence, it is worth noting that even an avowed atheist like Richard Dawkins is now calling himself a cultural Christian.[66] As with political liberalism, he is willing to adopt and indeed affirm the positive influence the followers of Jesus have had on this tired old world. But he cannot, at this time, accept or adopt the paternity and source of his beliefs. He remains unable to acknowledge or submit to the lordship of Jesus, but he freely acknowledges the influence for good the followers of Jesus have visited upon the so-called free West and world. More ominously, it might well be that *the formidable foe of Christianity* is closer to home than we suspect. It may be that the enemy of Jesus resides in the Church in various aberrant and violent expressions of the faith that seem to be devoid of Jesus at any level.

So, what then were some of the evils that existed in antiquity that are no longer with us because of the influence of Jesus and his followers on the world? What are some of the good things that Jesus and his followers have brought to this broken and hurting world that God loves so much that Jesus died for it (John 3:16)?

In *The Rise of Christianity*, Rodney Stark speaks of the infanticide of unwanted baby girls who were routinely discarded down the catacombs of ancient Rome because their society valued male lives over female.[67] Into that context, the emerging growth of Christian influence said absolutely not, we cannot treat human life as merely disposable. All life is given by God and returns to God. No, we cannot commit nor condone infanticide. The very fact that we are able now to debate a woman's right to access safe abortion, whether we regard that as less important or on equal footing with the right to life of the child being carried, *has its origin in Christian thought and praxis.* Mothers, as protectors and incubators of the life they carry, cannot ethically be more disposable than the lives that they carry.

The value placed on the lives of young girls and boys too was significantly increased through Christian influence. Child labour eventually came to an end in the West because of the activism of Christians. Gladiatorial combat unto death in the circus at Rome was not stopped because humanity came to its senses. It was stopped because the culture became deeply Christian and was convicted that this was not something that followers of the King should do to one another. Nor was it a thing Christians allowed to happen to other people, regardless of their beliefs. Gladiatorial combat ceased in 404 AD with the new Christian-minded empire of Rome. Likewise

Constantine I, who from appearances was certainly a Christian of a kind, banned crucifixion in 337AD out of reverence for Jesus Christ.

Stark tells how ancient Antioch, the city where we were first called Christians, was destroyed several times by fire and by plague. During the plague, Christians were driven by empathy and compassion to care for the sick and dying. Sometimes there were miraculous healings. Sometimes not. Sometimes there were long-term healings from the care affected by the carers. Sometimes the carers would catch the plague themselves and die. Sometimes the pagans would flee the city, deserting family and friends, and leave them to the care of the Christians who remained behind. From this general Christian ethic through the ages grew up hospitals, orphanages, universities and more across the Western world. From this posture and mindset came William Wilberforce and the abolitionists. Later came the emancipation of women, the vote for women, equality in the workplace, and more. All of this did not just happen because of the civilization or evolution of humanity. These things all had their origin in the person of Jesus and the Christian message, which we have called the Gospel of the Kingdom.

I am not asserting that these things were universally supported by all who claimed to follow Jesus. Not at all. Sadly, not even close to all. Often the battle for truth is seen in the battle that rages in the Church. I believe we may be standing at such a time right now, and it is in large part why *Bigger Things* is offered at this very time. But this much I know. There is evil in every age, including our own, however, there are many things in the world that are *a whole lot less evil than they once were* because of the influence of Jesus and his followers. Of course, evil is insidious and is with us in many forms that were not even in existence when the Early Church was born. The evil you and I face is likely as frightening as it is because with the advances of technology *we do not always understand what it is*, nor do we always recognise it. Discerning what is good and what is bad in modern times is not simple. There is likely no bigger spiritual gift required right now than the gift of discerning spirits.

Gnosticism has a fascinating link to both legalism and full licence to sin. In one form of Gnosticism, the adherents would move to stringent legalism, ***ascetism*** and bizarre forms of spiritual discipline like self-flagellation. A different form of the same underlying problem moves into complete licence to sin. Both these forms of Gnosticism are with us today. There is honestly nothing new under the sun (Eccl 1:9). Although ascetism is rare, various forms of legalism and tick box/performance driven faith are rife. With the advent of ***hyper-grace*** teaching, complete license to immorality is alive and well.

> ***Ascetism*** is a lifestyle of stringent self-denial and abstinence from "worldly pleasures." It is often a way of life that is followed for spiritual or religious purposes.

The influence of neo-Platonism in the twenty-first century Church is most evident in an escapist attitude that overemphasises heaven and eternity and underemphasises the incarnation and resurrection of Jesus.

Hyper-grace is a view that overstates divine grace to the point of a complete licence to immorality.

Neo-Platonism can result in an expression of the faith that tends to disengage with the world. In its worst form it becomes observable in separatism and ***sectarianism***.[68] New Testament scholar Tom Wright believes that Platonism has distorted the message of Christianity to the extent that large segments of the Church have become irrelevant as a result. Christianity, he says, becomes controversial to the world when God enters it through us in human history. The posture with which we enter it, of course, will say much about whether history will judge us kindly or with revulsion. *When Jesus and the apostles taught a Kingdom that was counter to the kingdom of Caesar is when Jesus and the Early Church ran into trouble.*

Sectarianism in Christianity is a divisive ideology that says only the sectarian group has the full truth. It disengages with other believers, and with the world, which is often seen as far too corrupt to engage with.

A Gospel that is only relevant to the afterlife is a very weak and partial one indeed. It is a Gospel that ignores the incarnation, the resurrection and their outworking in the coming of the Kingdom and justice in this world. Instead, this form of the Gospel longs and hopes for an escape. It clings to its salvation and hopes for recompense in the next life. In the terminology used in Chapter 4, this is indicative of an under-realised eschatology, which sees the Kingdom coming *only* when Jesus returns, or when we go to be with him after death. The world is seen as an evil and corrupt place to be escaped, rather than as what Scripture teaches that it is: a fallen world that *was created good* and is being redeemed by us who have been called as the hands and feet of Jesus.

PRAYER RESPONSE

Teach us, Lord, to live a life that affirms that all you created is good. Guide and strengthen us as we seek to co-labour with you in redeeming all that has fallen, in anticipation of the day in which you make all things new. *"You make beautiful things; you make beautiful things out of the dust. You make beautiful things; you make beautiful things out of us."*[69]

CHAPTER 10

PAUL AND THE CORINTHIANS: TO SHARE OR NOT TO SHARE?

"Do not give dogs what is sacred; do not throw your pearls to pigs. If you do, they may trample them under their feet, and turn and tear you to pieces."

MATTHEW 7:6 (NIV)

Historically we know that some New Testament churches were plagued by Gnosticism. Most notably, probably the churches at Galatia and Ephesus, and certainly the Corinthian church. It is highly unlikely that when the church secretary in Corinth went to the PO Box to collect the mail he said, "Ooh look, another letter from Paul, isn't that exciting!" Paul's relationship with the church at Corinth was tumultuous. He wrote at least three letters to the church, of which one has gone missing.

We know that because he refers to a letter previously written in the book of 1 Corinthians.

> In ***1 Corinthians 5:9*** Paul refers to a previous letter he wrote to the Corinthians. This letter, which preceded 1 Corinthians, is unfortunately no longer extant. How incredible would it be if we found it.

The need for Paul to write three letters to that church is likely indicative of the extent of their problems. The church at Corinth was plagued by Gnosticism. Paul's letters indicate that the problems that beset the city of Corinth also plagued the church. Amongst other things, there were claims of spiritual superiority, an inability to recognise or submit to legitimate authority, factionalism, favoritism, suing one another in public courts, abusing the Lord's supper by over-eating and getting drunk, prioritizing lesser spiritual gifts over character and love, drawing undue attention to themselves, and sexual misconduct that included incest. "Whacked" does not begin to describe the church. There was a wildness about the Corinthian church that seems quite foreign to most followers of Jesus today. Yet in all his writing, Paul does not suggest that they are not Christians. As an apostolic shepherd, he keeps encouraging them **to become what they already are**. He consistently calls them to maturity rather than to faith. They have faith in bucketloads. Faith is not their problem. Maturity and living lives that honour Jesus is their problem.

The phrase ***becoming what we already are*** is vested in inaugurated eschatology. It is a recognition that Jesus has already secured our future, but that we are still working out the reality of that future on this side of eternity. We are encouraged to live as citizens of the Kingdom Jesus has secured for us. To "bear the family resemblance." On seeing him, we will be just like him. This is not a call to legalism, but to becoming what Jesus has already won for us.

In comparing what was happening in ancient Corinth with some of the extremes of the charismatic world now, you realise that the temptation to excess has always been a part of the Church, exactly *because God does speak through his Spirit!* If silence was the order of the day, then dead church would be normative. Let the dead bury their dead. I would rather care spiritually for those who are alive but need anchoring than for those whose expectation is severely hamstrung. *A playschool is a lot more fun than a cemetery, but the pastoral work is far more demanding.*

When someone of the theological stature of N. T. Wright is invited to speak on TBN (January 15, 2025), that is mightily encouraging. He discussed how Christians can, armed with a robust definition of the resurrection, *endeavour not to live their lives attempting to escape from the world*, but rather to engage with the world in anticipation of the renewal of all things. Perhaps we can start being slightly hopeful that the tide has slowly begun to turn back towards the mainstay of two thousand years of what the Church has always believed and professed.

By the time we get to the book of 2 Corinthians, it seems that the battle with the problematic and Gnostic so-called super apostles had intensified and reached its zenith. In that letter, Paul gives us some guidelines around sharing the experiential.

CAUTIONS IN SHARING THE EXPERIENTIAL

Paul writes in 2 Corinthians 12:1-10:

> *I must go on boasting. Although there is nothing to be gained, I will go on to visions and revelations from the Lord.* ***I know a man in Christ who fourteen years ago was caught up to the third heaven.*** *Whether it was in the body or out of the body* ***I do not know***—*God knows. And I know that this man—whether in the body or apart from the body I do not know, but God knows—was caught up to paradise and heard inexpressible things,* ***things that no one is permitted to tell.*** *I will boast about a man like that, but I will not boast about myself, except about my weaknesses. Even if I should choose to boast, I would not be a fool, because I would be speaking the truth. But I refrain, so no one will think more of me than is warranted by what I do or say, or because of these surpassingly great revelations. Therefore, in order to keep me from becoming conceited, I was given a thorn in my flesh, a messenger of Satan, to torment me. Three times I pleaded with the Lord to take it away from me. But he said to me, "My grace is sufficient for you, for my power is made perfect in weakness." Therefore, I will boast all the more gladly about my weaknesses, so that Christ's power may rest on me. That is why, for Christ's sake, I delight in weaknesses, in insults, in hardships, in persecutions, in difficulties. For when I am weak, then I am strong. (NIV, emphasis added)*

Three things are apparent from this text:

1. The man Paul speaks of as having been to the third heaven is, most scholars believe, himself.
2. There are things in the realm of the experiential that are *too sacred to share with just anyone.* That being so whether shared as a testimony to Jesus or not.
3. The Corinthian church is caught in some kind of overzealous spiritual competition with one another. They were comparing experiences and grading one another as inferior or superior based on the apparent wow factor of the experience. In this super apostolic swirl, there was little integrity evident. *The evangelists were counting toes rather than people. Does any of this sound familiar?* Corinth and the twenty-first century seem to have much in common.

The super apostles among the Corinthian Christians no doubt claimed many spectacular spiritual experiences such as visions, revelations, visitations, transportations and more. *Paul is reluctant to share his experiences*, let alone boast in them. His boasting here is deeply sarcastic. The only reason he is sharing is because super apostolic and adolescent behaviour has forced his hand. Spiritual fruit in Scripture is nowhere equated with power, experience or revelation. It is always equated with character and love. There is never any need to exaggerate or to lie about any of these things. God's stories in us are sufficient just as they are. Visions, dreams and revelations concerning angels, Jesus, heaven, and more are common in the New Testament, and common in the combined witness of the Church throughout the ages:

- Zechhariah, the father of John the Baptist, had a vision of an angel (Luke 1:8-23)

- Jesus' transfiguration is described as a vision for the disciples (Matt 17:9)
- The women who visited Jesus' tomb had a vision of angels (Luke 24:22-24)
- Stephen saw a vision of Jesus at his stoning (Acts 7:55-56)
- Ananias had a vision telling him to go to Saul (Acts 9:10)
- Peter had a vision of clean and unclean animals (Acts 10:17-19 and 11:5)
- Peter had a vision of an angel at his release from prison (Acts 12:9)
- John had a season of visions on Patmos (Rev 1:1)
- Paul had a visitation of Jesus on the road to Damascus (Acts 22:6-11, 26:12-20)
- Paul had a vision of a man from Macedonia asking him to come to that region to help (Acts 16:9-10)
- Paul had an encouraging vision while in Corinth (Acts 18:9-11)
- Paul had a vision of an angel on the ship that was wrecked (Acts 27:23-25)

There should be no surprise when God speaks to us through dreams, visions and other revelations. But we need to understand that these *experiences are subjective and never mirror reality one hundred percent.* Our interpretations are prone to misunderstanding and misapplication despite whatever prophetic gifting we may have. In addition, the real benefit of visions and revelations are usually limited to the person who receives them, with occasional broader application perhaps to a local body of believers, a denomination or movement who are then *called upon to carefully weigh what is shared* (1 John 4:1).

> We should be open, cautious and humble about these things. Yet we are surrounded by would-be prophets who broadcast their latest dream on TikTok without caveat or any disclaimer language, often tied into the political sphere, as if God has called them to be like Old Testament prophets speaking to ancient Israel.

At best this behavior is grossly presumptuous and biblically ignorant. In the cases where the prophesy is held out predictively and it is (almost inevitably) just wrong, there is seldom if ever any detraction or apology. I could highlight numerous such situations, but my intention is toward the positive. *The aim is partially to call the church to order, but not to discredit anyone.*

The Greek word most used to describe New Testament **prophesy** is in fact encouragement. Any prophesy we offer now, which is not at least encouraging, is by New Testament definition not really prophesy. It is not just some form of positive speak though, it can and certainly does sometimes contain things of a warning nature. It even reveals sin, where sin needs to be revealed. *But even in that,* the community will be strengthened, comforted and encouraged by what God has revealed in the present.[70]

The Greek word for ***prophesy*** in the New Testament is ***propheteia* (προφητεα)**. It is made up of the words pro **(προ)** meaning "forth" and phemi **(φημι)** meaning "to speak." It is the gift of interpreting the will of God. It is far more to do with the will of God in any given situation than sharing predictively, although it clearly contains foresight.

When Paul says "I know a man in Christ," he describes this experience in the third person instead of the first person. When he then transitions into the first person in verse 7, we know that he is really writing about himself. In case anyone reading this thinks that I have "left the Spirit," let me clarify. I have been enormously privileged to have had many experiences in the Spirit over the thirty-five years of my life in Jesus. I am more desirous now than ever before of the presence of God to saturate my life in every way. My posture toward these things is just more understated and, I hope, more grateful and reflective of some humility.

It has been a special privilege to have had an open vision, numerous warning dreams of incredible accuracy and more. I came through Toronto with all its laughter and weeping and collapsing. I came through that season renewed and encouraged because I was already anchored in the things that have anchored Christians over centuries. To borrow dear old Eugene Peterson's phrase, I was "already walking a long obedience in the same direction."[71]

Experience comes and experience goes, but the one we are betrothed to, Jesus the Word, remains forever.

I share the next story reluctantly, and do so only to illustrate that I am not in any way anti-experience. Less than two years ago I heard a heavenly choir singing to me for an extended period on a plane trip from Toronto to Yellowknife. I honestly would rather not feel the need to share what I regard as holy and sacrosanct. I have shared some of these things with people occasionally, if I felt they might be encouraging. Mostly I have been reticent in sharing because there is holiness and sacredness about these things, and because not everyone who loves and follows Jesus has had these kinds of experiences. There are far better and more devout followers of Jesus than me—there honestly are, I am at best a tamed rebel—who have never had any such experience in the Spirit. *There is one experience in the Spirit I have had that I share with no one. It is too sacred. Not for all the tea in China.*

> Scripture cautions us at various points, like the text we are discussing, to tread exceptionally gently when we are on holy ground.

We are not in some frenzied, misguided, zealous competition here. We are involved in the things of our holy, pure, blazing fire of a God, who has betrothed us to Jesus. *To one bride and to no other. One bride and no other. Please be cautious. Please tread gently.* Matthew 7:6 urges us to caution: "Do not give dogs what is sacred; do not throw your pearls to pigs. If you do, they may trample them under their feet and turn and tear you to pieces" (NIV).

In describing his remarkable spiritual experience, Paul is describing exactly the type of thing that the problematic super apostles among the Corinthian Christians would boast, revel and glory in. His sarcasm here would seem to indicate quite a few cautions: one, the probability of gross exaggeration of experience; two, assuming that experience equates with God's favour; and three, that *not everything should be shared publicly.* Paul does everything he can to relate his experience without bringing glory to himself. Paul had kept quiet about his experience for fourteen years, and now he mentions it reluctantly because his hand is being forced by infant Christians. Our inclination is to ask what really happened to Paul. Was he carried up in the body to heaven, or did his spirit separate itself from his body and go to Paradise? The whole point of the passage is that if Paul didn't know, then we certainly cannot know! *Sometimes we just don't know, and that is absolutely fine.*

Immature believers can be tempted to visions and interpretations of their own making. They must instead learn to rest in the sovereignty of God. Paul emphasizes this point by repeating "I do not know" in verse 2 and then in verse 3. Speculation at this point is useless. Paul did not know, and so we cannot know. Whatever experiences we have in the Spirit are sacred territory. We would do well to treat them as such. Chapters 14 and 15 expand substantially on discerning collectively and on weighing the prophetic.

CHAPTER 11

VINEYARD, TORONTO, AND THE MISSIO DEI

"To participate in mission is to participate in the movement of God's love toward people, since God is a fountain of sending love."

DAVID BOSCH

The pattern of God as the one who cries out: "where are you" can be seen from the beginning of time. In the Garden of Eden, God seeks the humans after they have sinned against him. Through every covenant with Israel, through the time of the patriarchs, the judges, the kings, and the prophets, and finally culminating in the incarnation of his Son Jesus Christ, the pattern is the same. The Christian God is the God who seeks out humanity. Yahweh is the missional God (***missio Dei***). Just as God has sought us out and drawn us to himself, we are filled with the desire to take his light and life to those who are unaware of his great love for them. Can we, whose souls are lighted with wisdom from on high, can we to men benighted, the lamp of life deny?[72]

Missio Dei **is a term that originated from Early Church discussions about Trinity. It refers to God's overall plan to restore humanity and creation to himself through the sending of Jesus into the world. Essentially missio Dei sees God as the calling and sending God.**

We may rightly say that mission is not primarily the task of people, it is the task of the "calling and sending" God.[73] The missional God invites us to participate in his great mission as we co-labour in anticipation of when all things are made new. In both the preface to this book and the section on the miracle of the Early Church, I have tried to show that bigger than the tongues spoken and heard was God's intention with tongues. The bigger thing in that case was the reversal of Babel and the uniting of multiple ethnicities in the Ancient Near East and northern Africa for the sake of the Kingdom. *A sign points to something beyond itself; it is not the focus.*[74]

The bigger thing on display after the coming of the Spirit at Pentecost could easily be called a *missional thing, as much as it was a uniting thing.* In reality, the uniting of peoples pointed to an even bigger thing which was ultimately a missional thing! The coming of the Spirit at Pentecost united a group of former doubters and cowards and *catapulted the Gospel of the Kingdom into the world.* In that sense, the uniting of ethnicities might quite accurately be said to be missional. We serve a missional God. The New Testament is a missional document. It is in large part the story of how Jesus calls and sends a small group of potty-mouthed fishermen to follow him, and in doing so changes the world. In Matthew 9:37-38

Jesus says to his disciples, "The harvest is plentiful, but the workers are few. Ask the Lord of the harvest, therefore, to send out workers into his harvest field" (NIV).

> The ***missio Dei*** has a relationally Trinitarian base. Just as the Father, Son and Spirit send the Son into the world, so the Father, Son and Spirit send the Spirit into the Church, and the Holy Spirit sends the Church into the world.[75] The pattern of our God is both calling and sending. God is the missional God.

EARLY VINEYARD AND TORONTO

On Mother's Day 1979, John Wimber felt the Lord prompting him to ask Lonnie Frisbee to share his testimony at an evening service. This moment ushered in a period of renewal in the Vineyard churches. Wimber recalls, "Over the next year and a half, God began visiting in various and sundry ways. There were words of knowledge, healing, casting out of demons and conversion."[76] He goes on to discuss the bigger thing God was doing through the ways in which the Spirit was working:

> Then over the next few months, *hundreds and hundreds of people came to Christ* as a result of the witness of the individuals who were touched that night, and in the aftermath. The church saw approximately 1700 converted to Christ in a period of about three months. This evolved into a series of opportunities, beginning in 1980, to minister

> around the world. Thus, the Vineyard renewal ministry and the Vineyard movement were birthed.[77]

On January 20, 1994, what was intended as four days of meetings at Toronto Airport Vineyard turned into five months of almost nightly meetings across Ontario. From there, these meetings spread through Canada, the USA, the UK, Russia, South Africa, and Europe. The meetings were characterised by phenomena such as falling, weeping, laughing, and shaking. None of these were new to revival, in fact, the history of revivals is replete with such accounts. The Wesleyan revivals, the Great Awakenings, and the Welsh revivals all historically attest to similar and the same phenomena. One of the common threads seems to be that those witnessing these things have always asked "what does this mean?" Acts 2:12 records, "And they were all amazed and perplexed, saying to one another, 'What does this mean?'"

> What does this mean? What are we to make of strange phenomena, and things that are weirdly wild and wonderful? What is their purpose?

Accepting that hindsight is 20/20 and that when the Spirit moved in such ways, things seemed more than a little chaotic, I draw attention to just a few things with the benefit of hindsight. The birthing of renewal and revival can be like the birthing of a child—more than a little messy. The time of renewal and revival in Vineyard brought about positive and negative responses, which are still part of the mixed bag of good, bad, and ugly we wrestle with decades later.[78]

My own take on this time in our history is that the bigger missional things God was doing were the conversion and healing of many and the missional planting of churches. There are so many stories of much bigger things from this season. My own testimony was that all my experiences in that period were positive and drew me closer to God. The weeping, the laughter and the falling. I saw tangible evidence of bigger things in the fruit resulting from the phenomena. In a congregation I was pastoring, a woman had a falling experience. Her husband, a habitual wife beater up to that time, was so overcome by her falling that he has never again laid a hand on her up to today. Clearly, that was a way bigger thing than the falling. It was not even him who fell; it was her. But he was changed by the Spirit of God as a result.

Then I need to be honest in communicating that I also saw much evidence of silly and misguided human behaviour. When I was associate pastor at City Vineyard in Cape Town, there was a woman who I'll call Susan who always asked me for prayer. Without fail she would collapse into a heap on the floor when I prayed for her. One day I went to my pastoral colleague Simon van Niekerk and said "Hey, Simon, not a major train smash but every time I pray for Susan she collapses into a heap on the floor, and I'm not convinced that it's the Spirit." With a cheeky smile he replied, "it's almost certainly not the Spirit, it's more likely a 'courtesy drop' to make you feel better about yourself." And the two of us had a good laugh. Where there are humans, there will be human behaviour. Some of it is neutral, some harmless enough, and some will lean towards the destructive and even the demonic. But through it all, God is at work on significant and bigger things. I would rather face the pastoral challenge of discerning and navigating the good, bad and worse than quench the Spirit from doing any bigger thing.

The sum of the good that came from this time, the lasting fruit, the bigger thing, is seen in a movement that has grown to close to 2,500 churches in the world. It is shown too in the salvation, deliverance, and healing of so many individual souls along the way. My convictions are difficult to qualify or quantify, so I will not attempt to do so. I will however offer some—admittedly subjective—observations from that season in the hopes that in a re-imagined future, we will be able to do this better together. Please, Lord?

A general observation is that when phenomena are present, the misguided and overtly revivalist will come. There is no preventing it. They will come with Gnostic fervour and a radically over-realised eschatology. They will pour in from all four corners of the earth bringing an unhinged contribution to all that God intends to do. The problem is never with God, it is always with us. In hindsight, I wish there were a way to keep these sacred things that God sovereignly does with us away from the spotlight completely. I thought what happened at Asbury Seminary in 2023 was a good illustration of keeping what is sacred, sacred.[79] Sadly and more typically, some from within the Church profane the Lord's work when every phenomenon and experience is shouted from the rooftops and posted on social media to be trampled underfoot. Having come through the season that I call the back end of Toronto in South Africa in the early 2000s, here are some of my takeaways from that time:

- The phenomena were never the big thing. The big thing was and is the impact of the presence of God on people, whether visible manifest phenomena are present or absent.
- Abandoning usual service structures such as preaching and worship was not advisable long term. If anything, a call to Christ-centredness and content-centredness over

phenomena-centredness was needed. Where that happened, the fruit of mission individually and corporately was lasting.

- Where room was made for the work of the Spirit but did not detract from the overall missional call of the Church, the ***missio Dei*** was perpetuated.
- Where the salvation, healing, and deliverance which the Spirit intended to usher in were pursued, rather than a fixation on the phenomena surrounding these things, the missional fruit was lasting.
- Where active dissuasion from autosuggestion such as catchers for the falling was encouraged, the phenomena were authentic and tended to move to fruit and mission.
- Where the ministry became a ministry of phenomena, the missional outcome seemed to be a perpetuation of more groups who gather around the phenomena rather than around Jesus.
- Where people who came to witness what God was doing were already anchored into a long obedience in the same direction,[80] they were renewed by the Spirit and continued in that same direction. Where the peripheral phenomenon watchers came to see the phenomena, they tended to come into the front door and leave through the back door once the phenomena had ceased. For many who fell into that category, their faith seemed to be summed up as phenomena-chasing. According to Mark's Gospel, *signs are meant to follow believers* (16:17-18). Believers are not intended to follow signs.
- Lastly, a word of encouragement to the Church: in all of this, always look for the fruit.

English and Anglican renewalist Michael Green writes:

> The Spirit of God comes upon individuals to create in them a quality of life that would otherwise be beyond their powers. There can be no doubt from a candid examination of the New Testament accounts that the prime purpose of the coming of the Spirit of God upon the disciples was to *equip them for mission.*[81]

D.L. Moody, who was neither Pentecostal nor charismatic, had the following testimony:

> Two women would say to him regularly, "You need the power of the Holy Spirit." Moody reflected thereafter: "I need the power! Why, I thought I had the power [because] I had the largest congregation in Chicago and there were many conversions. I was in a sense satisfied." Soon though, the two godly women were praying with Moody, and "they poured out their hearts in prayer that I might receive the filling of the Holy Spirit. There came a great hunger into my soul...I began to cry out as I never did before. I really felt that I did not want to live if I could not have this power for service." Sometime later, Moody related: "One day in the City of New York—Oh what a day!—I cannot describe it; it is almost too sacred an experience to name. Paul had an experience of which he never spoke for fourteen years. I can only say that God revealed Himself to me, and I had such an experience of His love that I had to ask Him to stay His hand. I went to preaching again. The sermons were not different; I did not present any new truths, and yet hundreds were converted. I would not now be placed

> back before that blessed experience if you should give me all the world."[82]

Manifest signs or no manifest signs, the felt presence of God is there to a way *bigger purpose*. Our God is the God who is always comforting, always calling, always sending, always restoring all things to himself.

PRAYER RESPONSE

In your engagement with your New Creation Lord, and in anticipation of the day in which you make all things new; help us Jesus, to see and to participate in these bigger things and not to get side tracked by the signs that point us to you.

CHAPTER 12

THE TWO POWERS

"The true measure of a man, is how he treats someone who can do him no good."

THE CONTEMPORARY GLASS SOCIETY

This chapter was meant to be a fairly simple one, showing that there have always been two distinct and different kinds of power at play: *the power of the world and the power of the Kingdom.* I planned to then illustrate the difference between the two. The task has proven to be more elusive than I had hoped. In a rapidly changing global context that includes, just since the January 20 inauguration of the incoming USA President, sweeping and rather surreal executive orders and threats, deportations, ever fluctuating trade tariffs, and an Oval Office takedown of President Vladimir Zelensky, it is emotionally and politically charged territory of the highest order. I enter the space with caution. I have striven as far as possible to retain an apolitical posture. This is proving to be exceedingly difficult given the circumstances. There are incredible sensitivities around navigating these times.

The aim of the chapter remains the illustration of the two distinct powers at work in the world. They are far more different from one another than we generally think they are. There always have been two powers at play and there always will be, until the Kingdom is consummated. Any one of us can at any time fall prey to using the wrong kind of power, even when we come in the name of the One who we claim to serve.

> None of us is ever free from using the wrong kind of power to our own ends. In a world where much of our conversation revolves around dissatisfaction with the status quo, there is a strong pull toward philosophy and theology that seems to offer a quick fix to our unhappiness.

The wrong kind of power promises to meet our needs because we long for stability and for things to be set right. It is only too easy for us to be drawn into seeking solutions in the wrong direction. With that in mind, let's consider the two powers.

Thomas Oord writes that Western Christianity and theology has supported the view of a violent and retributive God. Usually, God's sovereignty is then aligned with this view of power. Oord describes God's power at work in the world as something significantly different. He calls God's power *amipotence.*[83] Amipotence is the overlap between *God's work and God's power, as God's love.* Amipotence, as Oord uses it, is a disruption to the standard account of power.

Northern Seminary professor David Fitch has done similar work. Fitch says, "if love is power, then, in the words of the Foreigner song, 'I wanna know what love is.'"[84] Amipotence pushes us to question power and pushes us toward wanting to know what love is. Fitch describes the standard account of power this way:

> Power as a *force* exerted "over" a person or social group in order to achieve an outcome as pre-determined by the person or group exercising the power. Power is "power over," and, according to the standard account, it is just the way the world works, and so there is no getting around using "power over." As such we have no choice but to go to work and get "the good guys" in control of this power and use it for God's justice and righteousness in the world.[85]

The understanding of power dynamics and origin as "force over" is very much the understanding of many Christian movements or motivations at present. At root it is the same understanding as those who would impose Sharia law in Muslim countries. The only difference is the interpretation of who the good guys are. The overlap between Christian and Muslim fundamentalism, aside from being deeply disturbing, is seen in the justified use of violence. Violence is equated with the righteous violence of the belief system or the deity being represented. This theology is ancient and has been the cause of innumerable conflicts and wars, not the least of which being the Crusades and the wars of the Ottoman Empire. A theology of dominion, power, and violence is seen in the rise of every historical empire from the Egyptian, Sumerian, Akkadian, Assyrian, Babylonian, Roman, Byzantine, Arab, Malian, Mongol, Ottoman, Spanish, Portuguese, Napoleonic, and British through to their modern-day equivalents. The use and abuse of the wrong kind of power is as old as history itself. Colonisation traces its roots to the use of this power. Oftentimes it carries the added belief that the colonisers are doing so for a bigger, ultimate good or cause, i.e. that the end justifies the means. *But in the Kingdom, the end can never justify the means.*

As far as Vineyard is concerned, our founder John Wimber saw the danger of power-based extremities as early as 1993. In his pastoral letter to the movement in June and July of 1993, he expresses our posture toward the temptation of using the wrong kind of power: "We want to avoid the extreme errors of triumphalism, dominion theology or ***theonomy***, though the Church clearly has authority to take back territory by making disciples."[86]

> ***Theonomy*** is a Christian based belief that God's law should govern societies and civil governments.

I am writing this section in the wake of the controversy around Bishop Mariann Budde's message to the incoming USA President Donald Trump just a month ago. Clearly there are diverging understandings of legitimate power on display in two entirely different responses to her message. Because of different understandings of power and its legitimate use, there are (at least) two versions of Christianity on display in the world at any given time. Our current circumstances highlight the disparity quite starkly. One type of power is seen in geopolitics, government legislation and hierarchical power of any kind. This same power can be seen when the Church uses the power of the world but identifies it as the power of God.

> The other power is different. The power of the Kingdom is seen in the apparent powerlessness of the Gospel of the Kingdom.

That stark difference is why we now have T-shirts that say "I'm a love your neighbour Christian not a storm the Capitol kind." There are, as Shane Claiborne says, competing narratives of what the Christian faith is fundamentally about and what our priorities should be as followers of Jesus.[87] It is also about prejudice, race, and patriarchy. Some rhetoric from within the Church becomes remarkably more dangerous and indeed even hateful. Again, how did we get here? The collision of "Christianities" is not new. Frederick Douglass named this reality more than a hundred years ago:

> Between the Christianity of this land, and the Christianity of Christ, I recognize the widest possible difference—so wide, that to receive the one as good, pure, and holy is of necessity to reject the other as bad, corrupt, and wicked. I love the pure, peaceable, and impartial Christianity of Christ; I therefore hate the corrupt, slaveholding, women-whipping, cradle-plundering, partial and hypocritical Christianity of this land. Indeed, I can see no reason, but the most deceitful one, for calling the religion of this land Christianity.[88]

What is new, and deeply disturbing, is that in the North Americas at least, some of this rhetoric now appears to have an evangelist for its cause. Despite this evangelist's expressed version of Christianity being miles apart from any measure of orthodoxy, he has in every way become an evangelist for the language that is trying to camouflage itself as

Christianity. Sadly, it would appear to be a version of Christianity vested in earthly power and violence, *and a version of which the New Testament remains totally unaware.*

When Budde stood in the pulpit at the Washington National Cathedral at an inauguration week prayer service and appealed to the President to show mercy on migrants, many believed she was expressing a biblical virtue. "Blessed are the merciful," the Gospel of Matthew recounts Jesus as saying in his most famous sermon, "for they will be shown mercy" (5:7, NIV). Others believe that she used the podium to make a political statement. Joe Rigney, a pastor, commentator, and seminary professor, took it way further than believing she misused the podium. He saw in Budde's words a sign of the "feminist cancer" that is invading the church. When I last checked, the gifts God gives us did not come in blue or pink. Clearly there are two entirely different Christian narratives at play here. *Which one sounds more like Jesus to you?*

We make comparisons with Nazism too easily, which is not always helpful. It is almost inevitable though because Nazism is, along with Marxist communism in the USSR, the killing fields of Cambodia, Apartheid South Africa, and the genocidal Croatian war of the 1990s, our most recent global illustration of the rampant evil that can arise from the abuse of worldly power. The misuse of this kind of power has a history of bloodshed and violence throughout the ages. Whilst wholesale comparisons of current rhetoric to the Nazi Reich might not be particularly helpful, *it would be remiss not to draw attention to the startling overlaps in the critique of Budde by Rigney with WWII Reich thinking.* The similarity in language, at least, is striking. We need to remind ourselves what happens if we do not learn from history. Hitler initially was able to avoid accusations that Nazism was anti-Christian through the use of ***syncretism***.

> The Nazis rejected the biblical Gospel as feminine and weak. Hitler had it rewritten by State Church theologians as Positive Christianity. Positive Christianity taught that the Nazi ideology of strength and manhood should be integrated with Nicene Christianity.

> ***Syncretism*** **is the process of combining different ideas, beliefs, and practices together to create a new belief system.**

In 1937, Reich Minister for Church Affairs Hans Kerrl explained that Positive Christianity was not dependent on the Apostles' Creed nor upon faith in Christ as the Son of God. Rather, it was represented by the Nazi Party: "The Fuhrer is the herald of a new revelation," he said.[89] After Hitler's appointment as chancellor in 1933, the Reich Church in Germany began reinterpreting the biblical Gospel to curry favour with the state. By 1934 a group of Church leaders felt the need to respond to the reinterpretation with the Barmen Declaration. The declaration rejected various false teachings that had emerged. Notably, Barmen affirmed that all life belonged to one Lord and to no other; that the Church could not change its identity and message to assuage prevailing ideological and political claims; that the State could not claim to become the single and totalitarian order of human life, replacing Christ; and that the Church could not surrender the word and work of the Lord in service to any national desires, purposes, and plans.

I am not claiming that Christians using bigoted and dominionist language are necessarily Nazis. But some of the overlaps in language and worldviews between the current expression of, for example, Christian Nationalism and the National Socialism of WWII Germany are becoming similar enough that they ought at the very least *to be sounding alarm bells to any follower of Jesus.* Any time there is a syncretising of the pure Gospel of grace as taught by Jesus and the disciples with a different agenda, the outcome is ultimately that we are left with a different faith from the apostolic one that has been entrusted to us.

As we have seen, these developments in the USA are not entirely new. There is a long history, both globally and specifically in the USA, of Christians becoming concerned around the apparent "weaknesses" of the Sermon on the Mount and the fruit of the Spirit type Christianity. Anytime that thinking emerges, it is clear that the same spirit at work in Peter and the disciples when wanting Jesus to establish his earthly Kingdom and overthrow the Romans is still alive and well.

> Our human nature kicks against the goads of the powerlessly powerful posture of the Sermon. We want muscular, manly men to enter the fray and to resolve the problem by violent means if necessary.

Here is a snippet of "muscular Christianity's" history in the USA:

> In its American form, muscular Christianity sought to counter the supposed feminization of the Protestant Church by presenting a more masculine image fit for a "strenuous" age of American expansion. Athletics became an important

> part of the movement, helping attract men to church and mold them into strong and rugged leaders. It was in part through the muscular Christian movement that Protestants overcame their suspicion of games and recreation and came to embrace organized sports like football, baseball, and the newly invented basketball as wholesome—and holy—endeavors. According to the typical historical narrative, muscular Christianity began to fade after World War I, just when America's sports obsession was ramping up. In The Spirit of the Game, however, I argue that muscular Christianity did not disappear. Instead, the 1920s are critical for understanding how American Protestants both carried forward and reshaped muscular Christian approaches to sports. It was during this decade, dubbed the "golden age of sports," that Protestants were forced to confront a crucial reality: They would not be able to shape sports in their own image, as the earlier generation of muscular Christians had hoped to do. If they wanted to maintain a place within the commercialized world of big-time sports while also upholding the moral value of athletics—the "spirit of the game"—they would need to accommodate and adapt.[90]

As mentioned in the preface to *Bigger Things*, much has been written into the dynamic at play between Jesus and the earthly powers. I have tried to stay focused on the bigger things God is doing and saying rather than taking long detours down rabbit trails. Hopefully, this short detour is sufficient to illustrate that a skewed view of power undergirds much of American evangelicalism as well as Protestantism. It is fair to say that this view of power has become the standard account of power in the North Americas.

The consequences of this view are evident all around us. Christian celebrity pastors falling into gross abuse scandals. The loss of any discernable compassion or mercy toward people who are struggling with various identity issues. Christians, breaking the third commandment with consummate ease, soliciting the powers of the state to install a Christian Nationalist government to accomplish their cultural goals. The installation of a "Christian" government would appear to want to take us back into a ***theocracy*** of a kind. Taking us back into theocracy would be the undoing of what Jesus has won for us.

The commonwealth of biblical Israel, from the time of Moses until the time of the anointing of Saul as the first King, functioned as a ***theocracy***. A theocracy is a form of government in which priests rule and govern in the name of God and by hearing from God. Sometimes this kind of government is seen in a model like the marriage of Church and state of the Middle Ages, with the duumvirate of bishop and king. The Reformation of five hundred years ago won for us the separation between Church and state that has been the identifying hallmark of Western democracy. Some currently seem to want to drag us back into what has already been won for our freedom, because of Christ.

For me, these things evoke images from John's Revelation and speak to a Church that has become drunk on power. "Power over," justified by the standard account of power as "our violent and retributive God" in action. Much of that thinking comes out of the so-called prophetic world who then back this view, adding further fuel to what amounts to a power-hungry mob mentality. John Wesley told a man with a violently retributive mental picture of God: "your God, is my devil!"[91]

If you think this is all overstated, let me illustrate. There exists a very commonly followed church planting movement, platform and methodology that purports to "plant it big," i.e. through a marketing-generated church community. "Instant community," which is no true community at all. This planting model then sets up the planting pastor in an allegedly apostolic office whereby he hears from God on behalf of the people and the instant community follows what he hears. Aside from this model having no discernable New Testament ecclesiology, it is a throwback to a different biblical covenant from the one Jesus has won for us. In an age where high profile leaders are falling like dominoes, if a model like this, which lacks the most rudimentary of accountability structures, does not disturb us, I am not sure what will.

Oord's word *amipotence* puts a spoke in the wheels of "power over" thinking. It is then my contention, supported by numerous scholars and thinkers, that there are two distinctly different kinds of power at work in the world. Worldly power wields power *over* people and groups. It is the power at play for example in government legislation. It is not necessarily wrong and has its responsible application, but it should not be equated with God's power. It is power over.

> Because the Kingdom of God is inverted and counter-intuitive to the systems of the world and human thinking, God's upside-down power always works with rather than over. With and among people.

The work of God's power is forgiving, connecting, healing, persuading, convicting, transforming, and reconciling, all in the context of relationship. Fitch summarises the difference between worldly power and God's power thus:

> Worldly power is always seen in control via manipulation, or coercion of some kind. *God's power is the way of love*, non-violence, mutuality, non-coercion, inter-relationality. God's power will not coerce so it requires a giving up control of worldly power. It requires persons and social groups to open space for God's power to work, discern God's power, and cooperate with God's power. This all sounds much like Oord's case for God's power as love in Amipotence which is why it is such a disruptor of the ideological hold of the standard account upon the imagination of present-day Christians, and for this we should be grateful.[92]

If we still "wanna know what love is," then God's power is God's love. God's love, or power, translates in us as authority. The power we will need to go about doing the work of building for the Kingdom is God's love. Love is the backbone required not to become a people of violence. Violence is the easy way. Violence is the way of the world. Our way, the way of God's power, is the way of love. To be a people of peace requires the power of God to stand, in love, in the face of adversity, to advocate on behalf of those who cannot advocate for themselves, to patiently endure persecution, to show meekness in response to hatred, to come as peace makers between warring factions, to love, to be joyous, patient, kind, good, faithful, gentle and self-controlled.

Scripture is stacked full of narratives where the submissive and inverted power and humility of powerlessness ultimately overcomes the power of the world. From Old Testament stories of David and Goliath,

Nebuchadnezzar's humiliation, Joseph and Potiphar, Moses and Pharoah, Saul and David, Esther and Haman, to New Testament parables of the prodigal son, the pharisee and the tax collector, the widow's mite, along with the Early Church's very real conversion of the Roman Empire to Christ, the story remains the same. The history of God's inverted and seemingly powerless power *ultimately defeats the injustices of the power of the world.* My friend and Vineyard colleague Todd Rutkowski expresses Jesus' posture to these things well:

> In a world steeped in systems of domination, Jesus presented a radically different vision. One that subverted the structures of power and hierarchy. His teachings and life lived consistently challenged the prevailing norms that elevated the powerful and marginalized the vulnerable. Instead of promoting domination, Jesus invited His followers into a Kingdom defined by humility, justice, and inclusion.[93]

None of the things evident in the Kingdom of God is ever power over. These things are all indicative of power (love) *with* others. *The bigger things are inverted Kingdom values and Kingdom power.*

- We subdue by submission
- We live by faith, not by sight
- We win by losing
- When we are poor, we are rich
- God elevates us when we make ourselves less
- By coming last, we become first
- We will be honoured through our humility
- When we are hungry, we are well fed

- Our wisdom might seem like foolishness
- The Spirit fills us when we empty ourselves of us
- In giving up everything, we have everything
- When we are weak, we become strong
- We receive by giving
- We find our lives by transcending ourselves
- We live by dying

This is not the way of the world. It is not the kind of power we are accustomed to seeing even in the Church. It is not a popular power. *But it is the posture of love. The posture of the powerlessly all-powerful Kingdom of God.* It might be worth adding a poignant Anne Lamott quote to wind down this chapter:

> You can safely assume that you have created God in your own image when it turns out that God hates all the same people you do.[94]

Scot McKnight turns that thought around and says,

> You can safely assume that God is recreating you in his image when you love all the ones God loves.[95]

I leave this chapter with a nagging sense of inadequacy. The two powers are clear for all to see and they are most radically different from one another. But as different as God's power is from the power of the world, it is *the* ***omnipotent*** power! God is the "all powerful" God. And his power—although all-benevolent love—is not to be trifled with. Beyond God's unlimited power, the reality is that all of us will be subject to various worldly powers *over us*, and we will also wield worldly powers *over others.*

Theologically, God is both ***omnipotent*** (all powerful) and all benevolent. His omnipotence means he is the supreme power without any limitations. His benevolence is as benevolent as his power is powerful. Perhaps, in the style of Oord's amipotence, I can coin the term omnevolent.

PRAYER RESPONSE

Whether formal authority by title, or authority "over" vested by other means, we earnestly pray for the ability to assume our posture and power from God with us and with others. Lord, would you have mercy on us? We are helpless and hapless in this regard. Would you make us to be the people of the Sermon on the Mount? This is not something we can do without you Lord. Teach us in this how to abandon ourselves to you.

CHAPTER 13

THE FALL OF SAURON—JESUS AND THE MI5

"The Towers of the Teeth swayed, tottered and fell down; the mighty rampart crumbled; the Black Gate was hurled in ruin; and from far away, now dim, now growing, now mounting to the clouds, there came a drumming rumble, a roar, a long echoing roll of ruinous noise. 'The realm of Sauron is ended!' said Gandalf."

J.R.R. TOLKIEN

Some stories of bigger things are not as pleasant nor as easy to share as others. Some stories involve spiritual warfare and serious battles with the dark side. The wisdom of sharing this story remains to be seen. Time will tell. It would help to read this story with a healthy sense of humour, because parts of it are so surreal that they are honestly funny. If you take a lighter hearted approach to this bigger thing narrative, it will be helpful. Some parts of it are also quite disturbing.

In 2014 when I stepped down from the church I had pastored for five years, my family entered the hellish season I referred to before. I needed work urgently since the bills were stacking up thick and fast. I had been a sessional teacher at a small, private Christian university from 2002, and so it was to them that I once again headed to see if I could at least teach a module or three to help plug some financial holes. The university was formerly the college from which I had gained my undergraduate degree. I am called to teaching, and teaching is my primary motivation, but that was not the main reason for me to seek them out this time around. As it happened, there were no spare modules or classes available for me to teach. The university was midway through a radical re-org that saw them moving from an expressly Christian institution to an inclusive university offering Christian-specific programmes. Many saw that process as a sellout in what had been one of three or four seminal spaces for Christian-specific formation and ministry training in the Western Cape of South Africa.

The university had been very poorly managed and had run into deep financial trouble. As a result, all sorts of visions that were never the original intention of the organisation had been entertained and promoted. From my vantage point, the original vision of my undergrad alma mater had been hijacked. No doubt others will see it differently. Because of their financial troubles, the organisation had opened itself to visions coming from the highest bidders and one such bidder was then firmly entrenched as the institution's CEO. He was by his own admission not a believer in Jesus, but his wife was. His wife was the owner of a large Christian publication in South Africa. She had become wealthy from this publication. My own belief is that this man saw the "Christian market" purely as a business opportunity. He invested R6,000,000—at 2014 exchange rates $600,000 Can. The deal, as I understood it, was that he would put the money into the university and then take up the reins as CEO.

I received a telephone call from a board member who I had known as a sessional teacher at the university at the time I was a student. I had mixed feelings about this individual, but I was desperate for work. The board member mentioned that he was aware that I had applied to the university to lecture again, but nothing was available. He asked if I would be willing to do some work for the board. I scheduled an appointment with this man and he shared some of the "dirt" on what was going down. Essentially, from the board's perspective, the incoming CEO had kiboshed the organisation. There were things afoot on the campus within the executive management, and between students and management as well as staff and management, with which the board was very uncomfortable. But they were unable to determine the detail of what was happening on the ground. I was asked to come onboard in the guise of being sales manager for the organisation. I was to travel the country—literally—in a small 1300cc half tonne truck, or what is called a *bakkie* in South Africa, selling the university as a preferred destination for spiritual formation to some of the largest churches and Christian NPOs and groupings in the country. My previous life in marketing and general management in the corporate world of South Africa had placed me well for the board to sell me to the CEO. The board member who approached me felt that I would be able to discern the real lay of the land.

I was under instruction to market the organization but always keep one eye on the campus and have my office door open pastorally to all who may need to speak. Essentially, I was appointed as a sales managing spy for Jesus. *Weird, but true.* I was desperate for work and accepted the initial six-month contract as offered. The contract of course contained nothing of the "spying for Jesus" portion of the job. After my appointment with the board member, I still needed to have an interview with the CEO and sell myself to him.

> My appointment as an MI5 agent was not yet a done deal. The board member had apparently done some kind of presales job to pave the way for me with the CEO. The presales job was soon to show itself as more of a hatchet job.

The day of my interview came and what followed was possibly the most surreal and weirdest hour of my life. I was introduced to the CEO, who went by the disparaging nickname of Sauron,[96] by some of the staff and faculty at the university. He sat me down and opened the interview thus: "Bob [not his real name] tells me you are very difficult to work with, but that if I can get past that difficulty, you are very intelligent and capable and might actually be able to do something worthwhile for us."

That was, *I kid you not*, his opening line. What Bob had really told him I honestly cannot say, but previous and later involvement with Bob showed me that his motivations were not entirely beneficent. Equally honestly, I cannot for the life of me remember my response to Sauron. But his opening phrase was the high point of the interview.

From that point on, it was all downhill. The conversation at one point turned to the CEO and his vast fortune. He said, "let me tell you how I made my money." He then regaled me with tales of how he had restructured the horse racing industry in South Africa and how that had made him a multi-millionaire. After saying that he was unimpressed by the fact that I seemed singularly underwhelmed by his stories, he emphasized that it was very important that I understood that he was very powerful and had made a lot of money. I mentioned that I really did not know how to respond to this unsolicited news, *and that I had a significant heart for the poor* rather than the wealthy. He would not relent. I was told again how important it was for me to know that I was dealing with a very powerful person.

The psychoanalysis going down in my head included concepts like toxicity, narcissism, sociopathy and more. Eventually, after he repeated the story for the umpteenth time, I responded with something along the lines of, "well Bozo,[97] I am not at all easily intimidated. If intimidation is your aim with this conversation, you have failed, but perhaps I should say just this to you: my family and I have been through quite a rough patch recently and we really need money right now. Since you have so much of it, *do you think there is any chance of a loan?*" Being a sociopath, he was totally humourless. He was dumbstruck. He stared at me and said nothing for a half minute or so. He twiddled his pen for a while and then dismissed me. I left the office and the university campus thinking, "well, that's the end of that, there is no way I am landing this job." The next day he emailed a six-month contract for me to sign. Please don't ask me why. I really don't know the answer.

I stepped into the dual role and tried to build relationship in the university as quickly as possible to get to the main point of me being there. This was not difficult to do, because people under tyrannical rule and oppression always need to open up to someone. Sauron had, as all sociopaths do, surrounded himself with minions and sycophants. The most notable was the financial manager who went by the sobriquet of Voldemort.[98] I knew Voldemort from our younger days when we had played club rugby against one another. Unfortunately, I was no longer allowed to tackle him. So much for my avowed pacifist posture.

One day I walked into the office to find the financial manager berating the sales staff, who all reported to me. I asked him, in future, when he had a problem with any of my staff to have the courtesy of conversing with me since I was responsible for them. I added that he would not appreciate it if I went into his office and tore strips off his finance team. I communicated this decently as a reasonable request. Voldemort slid off to Sauron's office, leaving a trail of slime behind. The two of them gathered and colluded around the cauldron. The CEO later called me into his office to inform me that the staff at the university was small enough that we did not need line reporting. He exonerated the financial manager and allowed him to speak directly to my staff. I informed him that I would feel free to do the same with the finance staff. This really was not going well as it related to the covert reason I was at the university.

> What was going very well, however, was that I was maturing as an MI5 agent. People were speaking to me with increasing openness. What they shared was very incriminating and included sexual harassment, predatory and grooming behaviour, and the outright sexual propositioning of at least three women.

Two women had come into my office and shared with me what was happening. From these reports, it appeared that both Sauron and Voldemort were sexual predators. The CEO travelled into the university from a town outside of Cape Town, approximately fifty kilometers away. A few younger women would occasionally travel with him. They seldom all travelled together at the same time. He would try to ensure that he had one of the women alone in his vehicle with him. He approached them strategically *one at a time.*

A young lady who was on the sales team came into my office one day and asked if she could close the door for privacy. The offices all had large glass windows, so the privacy was from sound rather than from sight. I said of course. She shared her story. It involved a direct sexual proposition from the CEO on the road between the two locations. She declined the advance outright, and the response the CEO gave was, "with a woman there is no such thing as no. Only not now." I thanked her for trusting me enough to share the story with me, and said I would hold it until I knew what to do with it.

A week or two later, a different woman asked me if she too could bend my ear. I said of course. She shared her story. It too involved direct sexual solicitation from the CEO on the road between the two locations. She too declined the advance outright, and the response the CEO gave her was verbatim, "with a woman there is no such thing as no. Only not now." At that point I knew we had enough to proceed to the board. Two reports independent from one another had not only shared the same strategy, but also the exact same phrase in response to declined solicitation. I telephoned my board connection, asked him to bring a recorder or notepad and meet me in my office after hours once Sauron and Voldemort had departed. As an aside, the financial manager had also tried soliciting a different young woman, but since the goal was to expose the CEO as quickly as possible, it was expedient to focus our attention on Sauron in the short term rather than Voldemort.

In the weeks following my meeting, my contract expired and I moved on to greener and more restful pastures back in the Shire.[99] The board member kept me informed of progress and the upshot was that an agreement was reached between the university and the CEO. He could leave with his reputation intact, but not with any of the money he had invested in the university. The alternative was that he fought for his investment but would face exposure and litigation from the university and the women he had harassed. My understanding was that the women had been consulted and had agreed that this was the best course of action given the circumstances. I was not necessarily in agreement with the decision, but my distasteful task had been completed and I had no say in the matter.

> And so, Sauron's reign was over, the ring of power was destroyed, and he departed sans his R6,000,000 investment. Middle-earth was safe again.[100]

Shortly afterward, new and functional investors came onboard and the whole leadership structure of the university changed. From what I understand, Voldemort too eventually departed to the hole from whence he had come.

Sometimes the things that we are called upon to do in battle for the sake of the Kingdom are neither pleasant nor life-giving. But the reality is that the occasion for spiritual warfare does arise. When it does, we need to enter it, not flee from it. There will be battles that leaders face that need to be fought. What I have not given detail on is that there was significant prayer surrounding the unsavoury task ascribed to me. I met on campus with various people and we would pray into specific situations. The university librarian—who is a friend from both the university and the Anglican grouping I was once part of—and I prayed together several times. There were other people and groups who also surrounded us with prayer.

> Sometimes, like King David, we are called on to participate in very unpleasant battles. Sometimes there is too much blood spilled on the ground, as 1 Chronicles 22:8 puts it, for us to reap the bigger thing that God might accomplish through the work of our hands.

In such cases, we need to move on to greener pastures and allow others to receive the inheritance we were unable to receive in that space ourselves. We are each merely servants who have our role to play:

> *For when one says, "I follow Paul," and another, "I follow Apollos," are you not mere human beings? What, after all, is Apollos? And what is Paul? Only servants, through whom you came to believe—as the Lord has assigned to each his task. I planted the seed, Apollos watered it, but God has been making it grow. So neither the one who plants nor the one who waters is anything, but only God, who makes things grow. The one who plants and the one who waters have one purpose, and they will each be rewarded according to their own labor. For we are co-workers in God's service; you are God's field, God's building. (1 Cor 3:4-9, NIV)*

PRAYER RESPONSE

Lord Jesus, you have taught us how to pray. In the prayer you gave us, you teach us to ask for protection from the evil one. We want to pray for believers everywhere that, when faced with the dark side, and when the time comes to engage it, the powers and principalities faced would bow the knee to you and go to your feet. We pray too that our posture would be to lean toward your light, to trust and watch as you expel all that is from the Satan and his minions in your protection of your bride, the one you are wed to.

CHAPTER 14

LISTENING TOGETHER IN COMMUNAL DISCERNMENT

"God speaks in the silence of the heart.
Listening is the beginning of prayer."

MOTHER TERESA

Over the years I have been part of many processes seeking communal discernment. Some have felt closer to attaining this elusive goal than others. Recently I was part of a communally discerned process of discovering Anida's and my successors as lead pastor(s) at Yellowknife Vineyard Church. I also currently serve on the team that has been tasked with finding David Ruis' successor as National Director for Vineyard Canada. This task has ended up being a bit of a reorg too, but the original mandate of finding an incoming director remains. Both these discernment processes have run over an extended period and have been prayerfully approached and communally assessed. In the case of

Yellowknife, the whole discernment and transition phase lasted close to two years and was completed at end March 2025. In the case of the Vineyard director succession team, the whole process will likely take about two and a half years. Both these processes have been life-giving and have taught me much about communal discernment, in which I was only vaguely competent fifteen years ago. I continue to learn.

> In general, it seems that there are two rather different approaches to communally discerning the will of God. Both strive to fulfill a clear biblical principle, but the approaches are quite different.

The three passages below illustrate the injunction well:

> *Dear friends, do not believe every spirit, but test the spirits to see whether they are from God, because many false prophets have gone out into the world. (1 John 4:1, NIV)*
>
> *And this is my prayer: that your love may abound more and more in knowledge and depth of insight, so that you may be able to discern what is best and may be pure and blameless for the day of Christ, filled with the fruit of righteousness that comes through Jesus Christ–to the glory and praise of God. (Phil 1:9-11, NIV)*
>
> *Do not conform to the pattern of this world, but be transformed by the renewing of your mind. Then you will be able to test and approve what God's will is—his good, pleasing and perfect will. (Rom 12:2, NIV)*

We all want to be able to properly and communally discern things like leadership successions, building projects, missional support, material changes in vision, organisational reorgs, or large capital expenditures, to name a few.

The first approach to communal discernment, and the one I was most familiar with before landing in Vineyard, looks something like this: A group needs to make an important decision. They follow whoever is leading the process and trust the process to take them where it needs to go. They pray before and after and during the process and entrust it all to God. It might include some or all of the following:

- We will run with a democratic process if it comes to that. The most votes wins. In the case of a tie, there may be a deciding vote
- Since time is of the essence, we will talk, think, pray and then decide within a relatively short time span
- Because we are praying before, during and after meetings we can safely assume God is guiding the process

The inherent weakness of this type of process is that the most vocal, persuasive, passionate, and more concerningly, just the loudest voices in the room tend to steer it. Whether it is a board meeting, an elders meeting, a finance meeting, or whatever other process, in Dan Wilt's words, such an exercise becomes one of "Christianizing" the process.[101]

Wilt suggests that such a process would seem to have more limited long-term results and efficacy than a more intentionally listening posture. He doesn't use the phrase listening posture but he intimates it. I would like to offer an alternative process that seems to be closer to the Early Church's practices of combined prayer and active listening to the Spirit in reaching communal decisions. Though even some of the practices of discerning God's will described in the New Testament might not actually be the best for them or for us! Drawing lots in Acts 1:23-26 to decide on Judas Iscariot's replacement, for example, might not have been a best practice for them and I certainly wouldn't regard that as a best practice for us today. In fact, this situation might well be one of those I referred to as *descriptive* rather than *prescriptive* in Chapter 3.

The succession team I currently serve on is the most intentional *listening* group I have been part of to date. We not only seek to hear God, but we also most fully, patiently and respectfully hear one another. And, surprise, surprise, when we feel we have heard one another, somewhere along the line it seems we are hearing God. Others outside the team affirm that they are hearing similar things. A process like this is very hard to qualify or to quantify in a "ten steps to hearing God" sort of way. It's really not an abstract thing. Our aim is *telos,* or outcome. We want to do this with God, and in community, *for* the Kingdom. We are practical mystics. But, in as much as these things are hard to quantify, it is important to try to do so to give us a framework from within which to move to communal listening exercises.

The aim is to make decisions within community in a way that amplifies God's voice above all the other voices that could divert us. And there are many distracting voices and noises that want to keep us from hearing God. This means we need an intentional, extended, and affirmed listening process that falls to a decision where we can say ultimately that it seemed "good to the Holy Spirit and to us" (Acts 15:28, NIV). It is not insignificant that "good to the Spirit" precedes "good to us" in Luke's writing in Acts. The sequence emphasises that the decision was not based solely on human desire, but that it was a divinely led process, which in this instance, led to the inclusion of Gentiles rather than a schism in the Early Church. Acts 15:28 reads literally: "it seemed good to the Holy Spirit and to us," *Edoxen gar to Pneumati to Hagio kai hemin* (Εδοξεν γαρ τω Πνευματι τω Αγιω και ημιν).

> Surprise, surprise, when we feel we have heard one another, somewhere along the line it seems we are hearing God.

The first discernment process described above, the one that assumes because a group is praying God endorses its decision, might have said it like this: "it seemed good to us, so we are happy that it's good to go with the Holy Spirit too."

Listening to one another, listening to Jesus, and practising mutual respect and submission to one another are foundational to the discipline of communal spiritual discernment. The following characteristics will be evident in such a process:

- The process is non-anxious and unhurried—we move slowly and thoroughly, seeking affirmation from the Spirit and others along the way
- We hear one another, trusting the Jesus *in* the other
- We speak what we believe Jesus is saying rather than come with our own predetermined agendas and beliefs. We try, as far as humanly possible, to come trusting Jesus, trusting the people, and trusting the process without the need to try to steer it
- We are mature enough to know that our personal discernment is not untainted since it brings little old me along with it

- We clear our hearts and minds individually and communally to make space for the Spirit
- We look to the ancient discerning practices of the Church throughout the ages

Communal discernment done patiently and carefully is a satisfying and an edifying faith-building exercise. There is more than ample evidence of it having been part and parcel of Christian communal practice from the time of the apostles and the Early Church. The sometime current practice of an apostolic figure hearing from God then acting unilaterally with everyone else following the "man of God" is in direct contravention of the traditional practice of the Church throughout the ages, and certainly has scant New Testament undergirding. It is in essence an Old Testament theocratic model. It still somehow remains the model of discernment in many places, despite the unravelling of so many leaders and organisations that practiced unilateral decision making without safety checks, balances and accountability.

> We need an intentional, extended, and affirmed listening process that falls to a decision where we can say ultimately that it seemed good to the Holy Spirit and to us.

The next section considers the *relational weighing of prophesy in community*, moving our thinking and our imaginations from the "one" to the "many." Similar, but also a little different.

CHAPTER 15

WEIGHING THE PROPHETIC[102]

"Let us know; let us press on to know the LORD; his going out is as sure as the dawn; he will come to us as the showers, as the spring rains that water the earth."

HOSEA 6:3 (ESV)

There are many more things I want to say to you, but your hearts are not strong enough to hear them now. When the Spirit of Truth comes, he will be the one to tell you. He will be your one true spirit guide and will lead you down the path of truth. He will fully represent me and will tell you only what I have told him. The Spirit will show you what is coming on the road ahead. He will honor me by making known to you everything I have shown him. All that I am and all that I have comes from the Father. He has not held back one thing from me, and the Spirit will not hold back anything from you.

-Jesus, in John 16:13, (FNV) First Nations Version Bible

JOURNEYING OF FRIENDS

We are on a journey. To follow Jesus is to enter a life of faith caught up in the adventure of obedience born of, and sustained by, love. "If you love me, you will walk in my ways. I will ask the Father to send one who will always walk beside you and guide you on the good road. He is the Spirit of Truth, the one this world is not able to accept because it does not see or know him. But you know him, for he is with you now and will soon be in you."

-Jesus, in John 14:15-17, (FNV)

To walk in this way of Jesus is to be invited into relationship, indeed, friendship. A becoming, together. The Way is a person. The Truth is a person. The Life is a person. Our lives are imbued and permeated with his.

Stanley Hauerwas says: "It's so easy to separate the teaching from the teacher and live as though we don't really need Christ, we just need the teachings. Everything is actually embedded in the person and the story of Christ. His story needs to become our story."[103] And this grand story goes all the way back to the beginning of God calling out a people from among the nations. Abraham's journey of faith shows us that belief in God is a living, moving conviction that is more than simply an acknowledgment of God—even demons do that with trembling—but an active friendship, for Abraham was called "God's friend" (Jas 2:23, NIV).

In turn, Jesus calls us friend. "Servants don't know the Master's business," Jesus says. "So, instead, I call you friends, for everything that I have learned from my Father I have made known to you, and that's what friends do" (John 15:15, paraphrase). We all know the saying: any friend of yours is a friend of mine. Well, there is still another friend that Jesus wants us to meet. He introduces the Holy Spirit to us as another advocate, another friend, that will not only be with us but *in us*:

> *If you love me, show it by doing what I've told you. I will talk to the Father, and he'll provide you another Friend so that you will always have someone with you. This Friend is the Spirit of Truth. The godless world can't take him in because it doesn't have eyes to see him, doesn't know what to look for. But you know him already because he has been staying with you, and will even be in you!" (John 14:15-17, MSG)*

Jesus brings us into friendship with the Triune. Their bond is marked by a level of sharing, transparency and vulnerability that is truly stunning. It is this relational exchange that we join as we surrender to the Love of the Father, the Way of the Son and the Work of the Spirit. In that eternal ***perichoretic*** dance, the Father shares all with the Son. The Son reveals the Father and shares all with the Spirit, and just as the Son testifies of the Father—in fact to see Jesus, is to see the Father (John 14:9)—so the Spirit testifies of the Father and the Son, who "searches all things, even the deep things of God. For who knows a person's thoughts except their own spirit within them? In the same way no one knows the thoughts of God except the Spirit of God" (1 Cor 2:10-11, NIV).

> ***Perichoresis*** describes the mutual indwelling and containment of the three persons of the Triune God: Father, Son and Holy Spirit, within each other. It signifies a dynamic relational unity wherein each person is completely present in and with the others. This concept is often understood as an eternal "dance of love" or a mutual "being-in-one-another."

And our God shares all with us. There are no secrets here. This is not a relational space that is crippled by co-dependency. Nothing hidden in a closet somewhere, no family trauma that haunts each generation, no black sheep, and no exclusive access to *a privileged prophetic elite.* "I call you friends, 'for everything that I have learned from my Father I have made known to you,' and that's what friends do" (John 15:15, paraphrase). And the "with us" and indwelling Spirit of Truth continues that unfolding work to this very hour:

> *What we have received is not the spirit of the world, but the Spirit who is from God, so that we may understand what God has freely given us. This is what we speak, not in words taught us by human wisdom but in words taught by the Spirit, explaining spiritual realities with Spirit-taught words … we have the mind of Christ. (1 Cor 2:12-13, 16b, NIV)*

> It is no wonder, then, that out of the wind and fire of the Spirit's initial outpouring after Christ's ascension, a prophetic people emerge. Their very existence is a statement, a prophetic signpost to the world that the Kingdom of Heaven is within reach.

The Gospel of the Kingdom is heralding the coming of a new social order—a new Way of life and being—a house of friends, where there is no longer Jew and Gentile, slave and free, male and female (Gal 3:28). It is the ***ecclesia*** of Christ—an advancing community that the very gates of hell itself will not withstand. It is a beacon of beatitudinal fortitude, a thin place where the Kingdom of Heaven has come so near that the sick are healed; those whose lives have been prematurely stolen away are risen again to life; the untouchables are released from quarantine, embraced and cleansed; demonic oppression is shattered and people are delivered from evil. No strings attached. No bait and switch. No deception. In the true spirit of friendship sustained by the Spirit of Truth, what is freely received is freely given (Matt 10:7-8). Walter Brueggemann writes that "the prophetic tasks of the church are to tell the truth in a society that lives in illusion, grieve in a society that practices denial, and express hope in a society that lives in despair."[104]

HERE COME THE PROPHETS

> *As these new followers lived together in peace, their harmony grew stronger, and they shared all things. Many of them had a giveaway to provide for all who were in need. Each day Creator sent more people who were being set free to join with them. (Acts 2:44, 47b, FNV)*

As the Church began to blossom in cosmopolitan cities far from the epicentre of Jerusalem, these burgeoning communities of faith experienced a vibrancy and creativity that could only come as the result of a Spirit-initiated intercultural, cross-generational grafting of a born-again new social order. Reflecting the initial outpouring of the Spirit at Pentecost, all peoples continue to experience the outworking of the Holy Spirit's power and presence. A tsunami of prophesying sons and daughters—young and old, men and women—from every tribe, tongue and nation are cascading out from Jerusalem. The ancient prayer of Moses, a cry that "all the LORD's people were prophets and the LORD would put his Spirit on them!" (Num 11:29, NIV) is being answered as sure as the prophecy of Joel 2 is being fulfilled in real time and in full view.

The outsiders, the Gentile nations, were now being grafted into the original and foundational Jewish stalk that had been the people of God for generations. This Gentile grafting, tapping into the nourishment and life of all that had gone on before with God's covenant people, was sprouting new life. The new social order of Jesus was taking shape. A new people, called out and sustained by the Spirit's work, were becoming an ***ecclesia*** unlike anything the world had ever seen. A deep and transforming work of the Spirit of God was at hand. Then the inevitable harsh winds of persecution spread these Kingdom seeds far beyond Jerusalem into the likes of Phoenicia, Cyprus and Antioch. It was out there, particularly in Antioch, that the peculiar and extraordinary growth of the Church amongst a predominantly Gentile population took form.

You bet this got the attention of those in Jerusalem. They sent Barnabas to investigate. Barnabas was "the encourager" and radical friend who had journeyed with the earliest apostles and taken Saul, the disciple-killer, under his wing and eased him into the church after his astonishing conversion. Barnabas was very encouraged by what he sees and experiences. The church in Antioch continues to grow. Barnabas needed help, so he went to find his old friend Saul, the "Pharisee of all Pharisees," who was struck down by the mercy of Christ and eventually called as a "light to the Gentiles." He wanted Saul to come and support this expanding work. Barnabas travels to Tarsus, finds Saul, and they both spend a year teaching and ministering amid this expanding Gentile community, where the name of Christian (Χριστιανοι) is first given. The term is plural, meaning "little Christs." As Willie Jennings observes, "Christian in its plural form always equals a strange new future."[105]

> The new social order of Jesus was taking shape. A new people, called out and sustained by the Spirit's work, were becoming an ***ecclesia*** unlike anything the world had ever seen.

And it is here that the prophets come. Into the complexity of the Church finding its way in uncharted waters of culture, expression and theology, the prophetic ministry arrives. Several prophets are sent from Jerusalem, as it is becoming ever clearer that discerning the voice of the Spirit is critical to the continuing journey of the followers of Jesus and their communities. Just as the church was birthed, so it would be sustained and remain an effective vehicle for the advancement of God's Kingdom on earth. Both in its gathering and its scattering, it is the voice of the Spirit that must be heeded. In Antioch, we find people who knew how to listen. From the prophecy of Agabus in Acts 11 to the council of prophets and teachers in Acts 13, *it is clear that the Spirit is not a silent One who only occasionally whispers into an individual's inner-heart*, but rather "a communion-bearing, community-forming God who speaks in the midst of the multitude and makes known where we must go to follow the Spirit's movement."[106]

From the warning of a widespread famine and the resulting call to the believers to be agents of relief and hope in the midst of it, to the setting aside of Barnabas and Saul for ministry beyond Jerusalem, and stretching even farther than Antioch, the Spirit was speaking, guiding, and leading. The voices of the disciples and the voice of the Spirit were synchronized. The prophets and the teachers were in lockstep. The discerning capacity of the community was increasing. Later in Acts 15, Luke coins a brilliant summation of this rhythm of discerning the Spirit's leading and the believers' obedience to it: "it seemed good to the Holy Spirit and to us." This is the way forward.

> Into the complexity of the Church finding its way in uncharted waters of culture, expression and theology, the prophetic ministry arrives.

CONCLUDING TOGETHER

The Church was maturing and learning to walk together in discovering what the Father was doing. Responding in obedience to Christ and the leading of the Holy Spirit continues to mark the expansion of the Church as it heeds its mandate to seek first the Kingdom of God. Barnabas and Saul were at the missional crest of the Jerusalem, Judea, Samaria, end of the earth ripples that Jesus predicted. After leaving Antioch, they travelled through Cyprus and into modern-day Turkey. Saul, now identified as Paul, joined up with Silvanus (Silas) after a dispute with Barnabas resulted in them parting ways. Paul and Silas head off on a journey which will take them through Galatia, Macedonia, and Achacia, establishing new churches in cities like Derbe, Lystra, Phillipi, Thessalonica, Berea, and Corinth. *Each step is marked by prayer and a reliance on the Spirit's leading.*

Acts 16 captures the dynamic of the voice of the Spirit's guidance in the expansion of the Early Church like almost no other story. The company traveling with Paul had clocked some 200 miles of travel on foot. It wasn't an easy trek. They believed that the Holy Spirit had guided them in a certain way only to discover that they were being resisted by the Spirit. Once they were heading to Asia through Phrygia and Galatia, but then were "kept by the Holy Spirit from preaching the word in the province of Asia" (v.6, NIV). Another time, they came to the border of Mysia and tried to enter Bithynia, but "the Spirit of Jesus" would not allow them to (v.7, NIV). What did they think they were doing and where did they think they were going? As Tom Wright observes, "it's one thing to trust God's guidance when it's actually quite obvious to do what's next. It's something else entirely when you seem to be going on and on up a blind alley."[107]

It is quite a brain teaser to think about the undulating path the disciples seemed to be taking in Acts 16. It would seem from everything we know about them that they would carefully have weighed each step. As was marked by the initial decision to send out missionaries in Acts 13, it was as they were fasting and praying that the Spirit spoke (v.2). Then why would the Spirit resist them when they stepped out? There is something remarkable about the voice and guidance of the Spirit as seen in the metaphor of *journey.* Our faith is not stagnant nor contained. Our path is always presenting us with one more step. One more crossroad. One more decision. One more opportunity to discern, to wait, to trust.

In the Acts 16 story, although it is clearly the same Spirit that was guiding them along the way, he is called two different names within just a couple of verses. In one instance they are kept by the "Holy Spirit" and in another it is the "Spirit of Jesus" that would not allow them to enter a place. This illustrates the reality that the Spirit of God is a person who is in relationship with Jesus and the Father, and yet is his own person and personality. He is not a force to be tapped into nor some form of static energy. To discern his leading—his voice—is to know him, not only to be aware of his presence and guiding nudges. We journey with him. This all must have felt like a test. The team must have experienced some frustration. It is amid all this that late one night, Paul has an extraordinary vision. The language is such that we can only assume Paul saw something with his eyes open!

Paul saw a man from Macedonia, standing at the end of his bed and begging him, "Come to Macedonia!" Well, there you have it. The capital "A" Apostle had an open vision. This certainly must be the clear direction that is needed. Paul needed to be a good leader and declare to the team where to go. *But Luke indicates something different*: "concluding that God had called us to preach the gospel to them," they got ready at once to leave for Macedonia (Acts 16:10, NIV).

Luke's word "concluding," in Greek συμβιβάζω or *simvivazo* meaning reconcile, carries the sense of something *that is united together.* The group arrived at a conclusion which was brought together, knit together or framed. This is beautiful imagery. Paul was not abdicating leadership at all, since his opinion along with his prophetic experience in the night would certainly have carried significant weight in the discerning process. But Paul brought it all into the context of *the team's discernment as well.* Luke was confident enough in this communal posture of discernment that he could say that they had "concluded together."

THE SPIRIT'S RAIN

I think we see a bit of a template emerging. One phrase that captures the essence and understanding of the prophetic voice we see taking shape in the Early Church's emergence is: the Spirit speaks like a rain rather than like a stream from a single spout. This allows for accountability, but it also breaks the power of the hubris that can come from being prophetic and mitigates eccentricity. Examples include John the Baptist, Agabus grabbing a cord and tying it up, John the Revelator caught up in the heavens, and even Paul's "I knew a man caught up" previously referred to in Chapter 10. This understanding of how the Spirit speaks to and through the community in Acts is evidenced by several things we hold to be true.

> The Spirit speaks like a rain rather than like a stream from a single spout.

TRINITY

The Father honours the Son and gives him the role of Logos, the Word. The Word becomes flesh. The Son ascends and is seated while the Spirit comes and speaks on behalf of the Son and the council of the Trinitarian Wise, the Triune God—not speaking on his own but speaking what he hears from the Son. He draws no attention to himself, but rather glorifies the Son. The Son turns all attention to the Father, doing what he sees the Father doing and saying what he hears the Father saying. He says if we have seen him, then we have seen the Father. He is the Way, the Truth, and the Life, without whom no one can make their way home to the Father. But wait! The Father then turns back to the Son. He gives him the name that is above every name. He presents the nations to him as a footstool. The Son, excited about the presence, power and work of the Holy Spirit, cannot wait to tell his followers about him. He says we will know the Spirit. He says we will not be afraid nor feel abandoned, for the Spirit will come. And then the Spirit, delighted to be present with us to empower and heal, takes no glory to himself but throws it all back on Jesus. Who then turns us to the Father, who then ...get it?

The prophet Ezekiel speaks of God's voice like the "roar of rushing waters" (43:2, NIV). I like that. Not a single spout, but rushing waters.

THE BIBLICAL TEXT

Chapter 3 considered our posture toward Scripture quite thoroughly. Vineyard holds it dear and central to our faith, recognizing that the word of God comes to us through many different voices. Still, the canon is truly inspired by the Holy Spirit. It is our codification of what we know to be true.

Even the story of Jesus is beautifully told in the tone and timbre of several different voices. The Gospel writers remember and convey it differently. Rather than four different views competing, it is the beauty of truth being discovered through four different people's experience and perspective of Jesus. In putting them together we discover who Jesus is, rather than by pitting them against each other and fragmenting our understanding of the Word of God to us. *Like a rain, not a single spout.*

> The word of God comes to us through many different voices. Still, the canon is truly inspired by the Holy Spirit. It is our codification of what we know to be true.

OUR EXPERIENCE

The Catholic tradition understands the role of the Church's history, tradition and experience as central to understanding the voice of the Lord to his people. It is the Bible and tradition that together form the rule of faith. We may not want to lose the baby with the bathwater. For those in the more charismatic stream of the Church, we know there is truth here. Many of us saw an adjustment in our personal theological framework regarding the presence and work of the Holy Spirit because of experience that led us to re-engage with the biblical text and to take another look—μετανοια (*metanoia*)– and shift from cessationism to a more charismatic understanding. Another thing we have learned is that God speaks through whomever he chooses, and the source may surprise us! The newest believer, someone you disagree with, the whackiest person in the group, your enemy even—any of these can speak the words of God to us. We should never become so fixated on one spout that we lose the wonder of the rain of God's voice showering down all around us.

David Ruis tells a beautiful story that brings these three elements of communal discernment together. The story comes from a village in the Bāgmatī Zone, Central Region, Nepal:

> In the late 1990s, a small crew of Vineyardite zealots trekked up into the Himalayans. It wasn't a ministry trip per se, but being followers of Jesus, their adventure couldn't help but result in praying for people and telling them the good news of the Kingdom. They ended up in a village called Nessing. Although they were young and spoke no Nepali other than a couple of basic greetings, they were moved with compassion seeing so many people who were sick and thus began to pray. They sensed some kind of impact, but it was hard to gauge given the cultural and language barriers.

In true Nepali hospitality, they were offered space in one of the small stone huts in the village and they bedded down for the night. As dawn was breaking over the mountain peak, they were jolted awake by forceful knocking upon the door of the hut. The door soon flung open to reveal a very agitated Nepali man waving his arms and yelling. They had no idea what was going on, and the only thing they could think was that this spelled trouble with a capital "T." After slowly piecing together what was going on, they discovered that the agitated man was none other than the village leader and a devout Tibetan Buddhist. It soon became clear that this man's agitation was not born out of anger as much as bewilderment. One of his roles as the village chief was that of healer. Wouldn't you know it, but after receiving prayer the day before, his daughter was tangibly healed of an internal sickness that had been plaguing her for some time. No more discharge. The pain was gone. Her stamina and energy had returned. The affliction's evil aura had subsided and was gone. The Kingdom had truly come near, and the future promise of heaven had broken through. All in the name of Jesus.

This had created quite a stir. They had never heard of Jesus, let alone interacted with him. Certainly, this experience of love and power was something completely foreign. Over the next months, and without any guidance or connection with the "outside" since there were no roads up into this part of Nepal, a church began to take shape. They didn't know it, but that is what was happening. Kamatasi, the village chief, had surrendered to Christ but found himself in a precarious position. One by one people were giving

> their lives over to King Jesus and the whole fabric of life and society in Nessing was being stretched in ways no one could ever have predicted.

This story made its way to David at least six months after it took place. His next trip to Nepal would most certainly have to include a trek up to Nessing. Bringing some friends along from the Vineyard community that was gaining traction in the city of Kathmandu, he was somewhat prepared to navigate Nepali village life, and through translation, communicate with the people there. The Spirit's rain had been falling. Jesus had been building his Church. The Spirit had indeed been leading and guiding people into truth.

Kamatasi shared three encounters that had helped shape his early understanding of how to navigate his and the community's newfound faith. One night he had a dream. In the dream the Lord came to him and told him that in his village no one could take compensation for praying for the sick. As the village healer—witch doctor if you will—Kamatasi now had to do this for free. Freely receive, freely give. Jesus' Father would provide for him. The provision which came from governing and leading was appropriate, but when it came to caring for people, particularly in the area of healing, he was to take no chickens, goats or food of any kind. Then he had some kind of visitation. He described something like an angel that came as a messenger from God one evening. The message was that even though he was the village leader, he could not declare that the village was now Christian. He felt he could remove the central Buddhist prayer flag from the village, but that he could not mandate that every household in the village remove theirs and become Christian because that's not how the Kingdom of Jesus works. Of course, if the whole village came to Christ, the story would have been even more incredible and yes, these things can happen. But for Nessing, it was one by one. Person by person. Step by step. Bigger things.

The third encounter was about worship. This seemed deeply personal, but the expression of rhythm, sound and melody that bubbled up was beautiful and communal. There were new harmonies and something very tribal. The Spirit was at work and songs of freedom were being sung. No one in the village at that time could read or write, so Bibles were of little use. The cultural nuances and differences were foreign to David. The poverty and harsh living conditions were also new experiences. It was all quite overwhelming.

During the ensuing years, the Nepali translation of the Bible has been critical. Literacy and education, especially among the younger generations, has allowed for a depth of discipleship, equipping and training that has been vital. Connection with other Vineyard churches throughout Nepal has been so important for accountability, strengthening and encouraging the community of believers there. But David was forever marked with an awe and appreciation of the role of the prophetic in practice, in seeing the church stabilized and mobilized.

LET ALL THINGS BE DONE

Let's continue with Paul on his journey to discover how he develops his understanding of the role and centrality of discerning the voice of the Spirit in community.

Paul gives us some of the clearest and most insightful guidance in understanding the Spirit engaging and speaking in a communal context in the New Testament in 1 Corinthians 14, specifically verses 26 through 33. At the time of Paul writing this letter, multiple layers of conflict were playing out in the Corinthian community. Significant division among members had arisen based on their allegiance to different leaders, with people forming factions and preferences (see 1 Cor 6). Essentially, they were prioritising human leaders over Jesus as the central figure of the church. Then too there were debates around sexual behaviour, lawsuits, marriage and more, all damaging the Lord's table. It's a mess. And it had become so bombastic that word had reached Paul all the way over in Ephesus.

Masterfully, Paul weaves together several brilliant essays which are collected in the epistle of 1 Corinthians. It is a wonderful example of practical theology. As is *all* good theology. Paul's instructions are born from the challenges of real life and living. The community in Corinth is taking shape as an incredibly diverse community that is trying to keep its bearings as it swims against the current of a bustling, cosmopolitan and vibrant city. What is culture, what is Kingdom? What is preference, what is wisdom? What is the Spirit, what is not? What is sacred, what is desecrated? What is profitable, and what is a waste of time and energy?

> This is not just illustrative of abstract thought; it is practical theology and practice for survival. In addressing the wounds that disunity has inflicted on the communal life of the church, an intertwined core emerges. It is the posture of love and the work—guidance—of the Spirit that will mend, sustain and empower the church whose head is Jesus himself.

One directive jumps right off the page: "Follow the way of love and eagerly desire the gifts of the Spirit, *especially prophecy*" (1 Cor 14:1, NIV, italics mine). Paul brings this central key of understanding right down into the nitty gritty life of community in messy Corinth. Paul has already made it clear that *love is not an optional extra.* It is the foundation of all things, not the least of which is the cultivating and engagement of spiritual gifts which are critical to serving and building a church that has Jesus as its head. The discerning of the voice of the Spirit is the linchpin.

> Paul has been laboriously unpacking this truth through the whole letter: the journey of the Church is not an individual sport. We are about something beyond ourselves. We have been swept into the glorious work of Jesus in making all things new.

Jesus is the head of this body. Love is the blood that rushes through our veins. And it is the leading and guiding of the Holy Spirit that moves every limb of us into acts of kindness, grace and service in this world that we are in, but not of. Throughout his letter Paul is dismantling the impact of social hierarchy that had been carried over from society at large into the formation of Christian community. It had been impacting the way they viewed leadership, how they interacted with each other especially in disputes, and it even marred the beauty of the Agape Feast. Where the Corinthians had become captive to the old-age social hierarchies and protocols, *especially* as they played out among the rich and poor, Paul is clear. This is not what is to mark the new social order of the Kingdom and the community that it shapes.

In addition to the social hierarchy, a hierarchy of "spirit"—πνευμα (*pneuma*)—over "mind"—νους (*nous*)—had captured the popular understanding of the body at that time. Dale B. Martin, a specialist in New Testament and Christian Origins, contends that Paul's disagreements with the Corinthians resulted from a fundamental conflict over the ideological constructs of the human body.[108] Entangled in the growing roots of the Gnostic tree within the Christian tradition, the Corinthians were in danger of their unredeemed social constructs informing a type of special and individualised role being given to the more mystical spiritual gifts. This gave a strange sense of elevated importance to the less educated among the poor and working class within the community and created collision and division with the more educated and wealthy. This conflict between spirit and mind was not simply about intelligibility but really about status. Paul will have none of it. C. L. Campbell writes:

> Paul's approach to pneuma and nous is thus consistent with his emphasis on the folly and weakness of the cross, which subvert all hierarchies (see Chapter 12) within the community of faith. Just as he had done with the communal body, so Paul does now with the individual body. He breaks down the hierarchy between these two aspects of the human being and encourages cooperation between them so that genuinely spiritual speech may also be intelligible within the community. This dynamic, cooperative relationship between pneuma and nous guides the prophecy that builds up the Body of Christ.[109]

Riffing off the "priesthood of all believers," Campbell coins the phrase "the prophethood of all believers."[110] The prophetic work is that of the entire community in rhythm and grace together. *We are a prophetic people—a prophetic presence—alive and vibrant, animated by the presence of the power of the Holy Spirit in and among us.* As the diamond of God's revelatory work is dancing and spinning at the heart of the gathered community, each one contributes a hymn, a lesson, a revelation, a tongue, an interpretation—*let all be done*—with the end goal (telos) of

God being worshipped, heard, and responded to, where all—believer and enquirer alike—fall on their faces and proclaim, "God is really here!"

> So, Paul gives the following exhortation as the central emphasis in holding the community on point, on mission, if you will: "follow the way of love and eagerly desire gifts of the Spirit, *especially prophecy*" (1 Cor 14:1, NIV, italics mine).

This is the God-given wisdom, discernment, perspective and teaching that the church badly needs if it is to go forward instead of spinning in a whirlpool of opinions, preferences and selfish agendas. The church Jesus builds is a called-out community of people, not simply an accidental collection of private individuals. We need direction.

PROPHECY

The prophetic has often been described as a multi-faceted diamond. Jewelers use the term fire to refer to the way the light bends as it passes through a diamond and results in multiple colours and brilliance. As the revelatory light of the Spirit shines on the Church, the results can be breathtaking. The brilliance, beauty and multifaceted firelight that takes form is wonderful. As Paul notes, when the prophetic is functioning and healthy in a community, it evokes a response from even unbelievers or enquirers, who fall and worship God, exclaiming "God is really among you!" It is a spiritual gift given us that we may discern and disseminate what God is speaking to and through the community for the stabilizing and strengthening of the whole.

At times it takes the form of preaching and teaching. This is not so much spontaneous as coupled with prayer, preparation, study and a measure of sobriety. Charles Spurgeon said, "The moment the church of God shall despise the pulpit, God will despise her."[111] Among the contemplative mystics and the more Pentecostal and charismatic traditions however, there is room for a much wider understanding of how the Spirit speaks to us in the present. Impressions, prompts, dreams and visions are but a few of the ways that the Spirit of God gets our attention. The Spirit enters our current reality and gives illumination into decisions, next steps and navigating what is yet to come. The more mystical aspects of this gift can create some discomfort. But it is important to have a keen awareness that it is part of the package of becoming and *being a prophetic people*. The very nature of "God speaking to us through us" is peculiar from the outset.

I hope by now the point is getting across. *Visions and revelations happen.* Wonderful, uplifting, exalted spiritual states occur. They are in a different league altogether from the states of mind that most of us experience most of the time. They are real and magnificent gifts of God, marvelously encouraging, a real taste of paradise itself. *But they are not given to people in order to make them special.* To think like that is to fly way too high, to forget that, in this life, "the wings are always fastened on with wax."[112]

There are some in the community that do, and will, experience things that are quite remarkable and unusual. To write them off as whacky or weird only hurts the community and discounts some of the wonderful spice and colour that this aspect of the prophetic brings into our faith life together. Many in the church who have such experiences have been needlessly marginalised and wounded. Sometimes, something the Lord might really have been trying to say gets lost and unheeded, to the detriment of the wider community, because we marginalise these things. We need to bring the peripheral prophets back into community rather than pushing them further toward the periphery where so many seem currently to reside.

> There is room for a much wider understanding of how the Spirit speaks to us in the present.

Yet prophetic or mystical eccentricity is not a free pass. It is not to be despised, nor is it to be elevated. Too high an elevation of the mystical has allowed for some unhealthy, and frankly damaging, practices. Excusing unwise and unhealthy behavior because "that's just them" misses the need for ongoing transformation, maturity, discipleship and accountability.

At the core, the prophetic gift is given to strengthen, encourage and comfort the community of faith. But this should not be interpreted as coddling positive confessions or non-negative words. In one of his later letters to his young disciple Timothy, Paul writes, "the time will come when people will not put up with sound doctrine. Instead, to suit their own desires, they will gather around them a great number of teachers [prophets] to say what their itching ears want to hear" (2 Tim 4:3, NIV). One of the key components of our National Team in Vineyard Canada is what we call a "listening team." On a regular basis, we glean from across the grassroots of our communities things that we sense that the Spirit is speaking to us not only in our localised settings, but as a national family. The Spirit will always lead and guide us into truth—and the truth will set us free. The most used word for truth in the New Testament—αληθεια (*aletheia*; truth)—means to be truthful more than having knowledge. It is perceiving what is reality and what is dependable. It speaks of authenticity, genuineness and that which is non-duplicitous.

At a Society of Vineyard Scholars meeting some years back, someone asked Stanley Hauerwas for advice on how to be a community that actually walks out a life together as followers of Jesus. His answer was: *"Don't lie to each other."* Becoming a people who tell each other the truth is no small feat. It requires love for each other, great courage, hope, trust, unity, freedom, and equality. Truth-telling takes practice. Over time, faithfulness to those practices creates habits. And sustaining those habits leads to formation as persons and communities capable of being truth-tellers, creating truth-tellers, and being known in our broader communities as truth-tellers.

> The prophetic gift is given to strengthen, encourage and comfort the community of faith.

So, Paul writes into the chaos that the believers must let everything be done in an orderly way. He shares, "I will pray with my spirit, but I will pray with my mind also; I will sing praise with my spirit, but I will sing praise with my mind also" (1 Cor 14:15, ESV). He takes the "most desired" gift of prophecy and plops it right down in the heart of the community with the claim that when it's all said and done, "you can all prophecy, one by one" (v.31).

TIME TO DISCERN

As critical and central as the prophetic gift is to the Church, it can be a source of disorientation and distraction, to the point that it can become disdained and treated with contempt. In Paul's earliest epistle, a letter to the Thessalonian believers, the role of prophesy had seemingly fallen into ill repute and even been despised by some. "Do not put out the Spirit's fire," Paul warns in his closing remarks in 1 Thessalonians 5:19, "and don't treat prophecies with contempt." Just as Paul links prophesy with the fire of the Spirit in this early letter, so he continues to highlight its key role in the Church when he writes to his Corinthian brothers and sisters years later.

Despising prophecy can take several different shapes. The more practical and studious aspects of prophesying can easily be relegated to the "been there, done that" category and not be taken seriously. Some may feel that they don't need anyone to teach them anything anymore because no one is saying anything new or fresh. This sentiment can arise in the one prophesying or in those who are hearing. Nonetheless, the outcome is the same: "we don't need that communal gift—I have my own personal revelation, 'truth' if you will." A couple in their sixties who had been Christians for decades left a church I was pastoring based on this perspective. They wanted church meetings to be only spaces of prayer and fellowship without any proclamation at all. I asked whether they had always felt that way and they replied that in their early days they were like sponges absorbing the teaching eagerly. I asked if it would be fair to other younger believers to deny them the same season of absorbing like sponges. Although it got them to thinking, they still moved on. A pastoral colleague and friend went to visit them in their new place of worship. I asked him what his experience had been. He said, "it was like being at a séance." The more eccentric and mystical aspects of the gift can go awry and lose credibility, as we have already considered in Chapters 9 and 10. With loose moorings to intelligent, prayerful discernment and the *tried-and-true* narrative of Scripture, the prophetic pen can become a hotbed of all kinds of zaniness and Gnostic buffoonery.

So Paul writes to the Corinthians, "Two or three prophets should speak, and the others should weigh carefully what is said. And if a revelation comes to someone who is sitting down, the first speaker should stop. For you can all prophesy in turn so that everyone may be instructed and encouraged. The spirits of prophets are subject to the control of prophets. For God is not a God of disorder but of peace—as in all the congregations of the Lord's people" (1 Cor 14:29-30, NIV). Along with basically "keeping it real" both in content and in posture, one of the biggest keys is simply *to listen well*, which includes making room for multiple voices to be heard. It is quite cheeky that Paul's instruction here is to say that the one who is mid-stream pontificating—bringing the "word of the Lord"—is the one who is to stop if interrupted. Hilarious! Now, Paul makes it clear in his musings that this is all done decently and in order, but nonetheless, the point is clear. *Sometimes we just need to shut up.* As someone who has spent their entire faith journey in and around churches that would all identify as evangelical, it is my heartfelt conviction that we have been far too quick to speak and almost unbelievably poor at listening.

> *I have a lot more to say about this, but it is hard to get it across to you since you've picked up this bad habit of not listening. By this time, you ought to be teachers yourselves, yet here I find you need someone to sit down with you and go over the basics on God again, starting from square one—baby's milk, when you should have been on solid food long ago! Milk is for*

> *beginners, inexperienced in God's ways; solid food is for the mature, who have some practice in telling right from wrong. (Heb 5:11-14, MSG)*

> *Do not quench the Spirit. Do not treat prophecies with contempt but test them all; hold on to what is good, reject every kind of evil. (1 Thess 5:19-22, NIV)*

This all requires a weighing—οι αλλοι διακρινετωσαν (let the others judge)—from those listening to determine if it really is of the Spirit or not.

> At times in the Vineyard, we have taken a lot of heat for posturing things like, "I feel the Lord is saying" or "I believe that God may be speaking." This is where we are most comfortable, however: clear, unabashed, yet humble and submitting. We hold a posture that we have come to describe as being "naturally supernatural." At the heart of this understanding is the humility and meekness required to make room for the other. It is not simply about the delivery, it is about the posture of the messenger themselves.

Paul knew all about rich and varied spiritual experiences, visions and revelations. He spoke in tongues more than all the Corinthians (1 Cor 14:18) but chose to speak ordinary languages in church so that others would be built up in *faith*. Though he had spiritual experiences of all sorts, he knew that the important point was not his spirituality—let alone any power that might give him—but God's grace. He had discovered that there was a different kind of strength, the kind that's really worth having, and that to possess it one must be weak.

Paul addresses elitism at Colossae too:

> *Do not let anyone who delights in false humility and the worship of angels disqualify you. Such a person also goes into great detail about what they have seen; they are puffed up with idle notions by their unspiritual mind. They have lost connection with the head, from whom the whole body, supported and held together by its ligaments and sinews, grows as God causes it to grow. (Col 2:18-19, NIV)*

Watch out, Paul says. One can become "puffed up"—*phusioō* (φυσιοω), "to inflate, blow up"—which not only speaks of the proud nature of the individual, but also the exaggeration and inflating of truth that accompanies the telling. It all gets blown out of proportion with the tragic result that it ends up disqualifying the community. "The Lord has shown me" can be code for "He hasn't shown you, so you need what I've got." This often seems to be the higher *reason* that comes as normative in Gnostic spaces. Paul describes their higher reason simply as *carnal* and observes that although these people make you feel like you're not as connected to Jesus as they are, they are actually the ones who are disconnected from Christ and his body. *Lord have mercy on us.*

JESUS IS KNOCKING

One of the most provocative scenes in the book of Revelation is that of Jesus standing outside the door of the Church knocking. This image captures the essence of the place of—and need for—communal hearing. A watching to notice when we have drifted from the way of Jesus and the wisdom to know how and when to encourage the church to stay on the path before us. There's an old Wimberism which seems quite appropriate here—"the way in is the way on."

The city of Laodicea was a bustling, successful urban centre checking all the boxes as to what it meant to be a player in the socioeconomic structures of the Roman Empire. It was a place of regional banking, finance, trade, manufacturing, textile production, and to top it all off, a medical centre. To put it bluntly, it was a place of privilege, wealth and power. The community of believers within this city had become quite accommodating of Laodicea's status, beginning to adopt it as a metric of measuring their own success as kingdom people. *They were enjoying some cultural buoyancy.* And it was eroding the core of their faith in Christ. This all left a very bad taste in Jesus' mouth.

Jesus says to them through John, "You say, 'I am rich; I have acquired wealth and do not need a thing.' But you do not realize that you are wretched, pitiful, poor, blind and naked" (Rev 3:17). Then he challenges them to find true treasure—gold—that is refined by fire. By suffering. The posture of Jesus here is remarkable. He stands at the door and knocks. There is a look and a listen here. Yet, we must respond and invite. Given that the city of Laodicea was a regional powerhouse, it is not inconceivable that this congregation was overly accommodated to the socioeconomic structures of the Roman imperium. Likely, having achieved worldly success, they had become assimilated into the guilds which were networked with the imperial cults and become entrenched in the social realities of Roman-controlled Asia Minor. Gregory Beale writes:

> That some kind of boast about material welfare is in mind is likely from the observation that wherever [plousios] ("rich") and [plouteō] ("I am rich") are used negatively in Revelation, the reference is to unbelievers who have prospered materially because of their willing intercourse with the ungodly world system (6:15; 13:16; 18:3, 15, 19).

> The same idea is present here. Indeed, this church is on the brink of becoming identified with such an ungodly system, as the second part of 3:17 bears out.[113]

The Laodiceans are counseled "to buy from me gold refined by fire" (3:18a). This reference is likely to the fire experienced by another of the seven churches of the Revelation, Smyrna. In the church of Smyrna's case, civil, governmental, and political agents sought to throw them into jail precisely *because of their faithful witness*. Such fire is fed not by divine wrath but by countercultural messianic discipleship. Obtaining, retaining, and expanding what Jesus considers as real wealth is costly in that sense, and so is following the Jesus path.

> The promise Jesus gives those who follow his path is not health, wealth, and prosperity in this life, particularly not if that compromises discipleship in the way of the slain Lamb, but rather, his presence, by his spirit, in our efforts to bear faithful witness to the world.[114]

We need JESUS. "Long ago, at many times and in many ways, God spoke to our fathers by the prophets, but in these last days he has spoken to us by his Son, whom he appointed the heir of all things, through whom also he created the world (Heb 1:1-3, ESV)." He is the beginning and the end—the Alpha and Omega. He is the ***Melech Ha Olam***—the King of the Universe.

> *The one who comes from above is above all; the one who is from the earth belongs to the earth, and speaks as one from the earth. The one who comes from heaven is above all. He*

> *testifies to what he has seen and heard, but no one accepts his testimony. Whoever has accepted it has certified that God is truthful. For the one whom God has sent speaks the words of God, for God gives the Spirit without limit. The Father loves the Son and has placed everything in his hands. Whoever believes in the Son has eternal life, but whoever rejects the Son will not see life, for God's wrath remains on them. (John 3:31-36, NIV)*

He has the final say. He *is* the final word.

From the *Book of Common Prayer*, for the Day of Pentecost:

> The Lord will pour out his Spirit upon all flesh,
> **And your sons and daughters shall prophesy.**
> Your old men shall dream dreams,
> **And your young men shall see visions.**
> You shall know that the Lord is in the midst of his people,
> **That he is the Lord and there is none else.**
> And it shall come to pass
> **That everyone who calls on the Name of the Lord shall be saved.**[115]

CHAPTER 16

TURN: BEGRUDGING ACCEPTANCE

"The greatest danger in times of turbulence is not the turbulence—it is to act with yesterday's logic."

PETER DRUCKER

For those old enough to remember, the Byrds had a hit with the song "Turn, Turn, Turn" in 1965. The song was based on the third chapter of Ecclesiastes. In a way, the title of the song describes what God has called me to over twenty-five years. Somehow, the call has always been to spaces and places that were at the very least challenged or, more often, in a degree of trouble or were literally "up shit creek without a paddle."

When the first church call to St. Barnabas came in 2002, many people questioned our wisdom in accepting it. At the time of the call, my family and I had been in fellowship in a Baptist church, and they mistakenly thought that I might end up as a Baptist pastor. That really would not have worked. We were even interviewed as a couple by the Baptist Union in South Africa with a view to accreditation in that stream. One of the interviewers asked Anida rather condescendingly, "tell me, my dear, how are you doing in the area of submission?" She responded, "well I have been trying for fifteen years, but he refuses to submit." The outgoing pastor of that Baptist church had said that I would pick up a good four to five hundred strong Baptist congregation with no problem. As he put it, "my gift mix" and strong teaching motivation were perfectly suited to doing so. No one really saw me going to a struggling inner city Anglican church with a team that was to bring renewal to that tiny thirty something strong congregation. I was seen as "far too big" for a role like that. The question begs, too big a what? We can leave the question unanswered.

In the same way, when we were called to Kenilworth Vineyard Church in 2009, it was a church that no other leader seemed willing to touch with a barge pole. The church was in conflict and crisis in every way imaginable. It was full of factions, conflicts, strong wills and characters. Additionally, a significant portion of the congregation were rather unteachable. It is not possible really to teach into a context where people think they know everything. As with the call to Barneys, albeit for very different reasons and in different ways, the task was one of turning the church around.

Some years after laying down the call there, I secured a turnaround contract with the Evangelical Seminary of Southern Africa (ESSA) with a view to assisting them in regaining their South African Qualifications Authority (SAQA) accreditation which they had lost due to bad management practices. Once again, the call was to a space and place that needed turnaround change. By this time, it had begun to dawn on me that the call to turnaround change was somehow on me, and as much as I tried to run from it, it could not be escaped. Call me a slow learner.

When called to Yellowknife Vineyard Church in 2018, that too was a space that had just seen five very difficult years. The church was no longer in crisis, and other leaders had done much foundation laying that allowed God to build a far more team-oriented lead under my spiritual care than had been the case in the past. However, the task was still one of turnaround. And turn it around God did!

In all these places of difficulty, ranging from challenged to total chaos, by the time of leaving, those places were mostly in a healthier state than when the invitation was extended to be part of their future. Some more so than others. Barneys was a success story in every way. A church that would likely have died still flourishes. ESSA regained their SAQA accreditation and is a small but functional seminary in South Africa under good leadership. Yellowknife Vineyard Church doubled in size and now flourishes under a new and diverse team lead, as probably the largest congregation in the North West Territories of Canada. Kenilworth Vineyard Church (KVC) was a less encouraging story. Its legacy lives on in two ministries it founded. One is *Ikhayalethemba* (meaning the home of hope) that was established prior to me being called as lead pastor.[116] The other is Mercy Vineyard Church, which was planted out of KVC while I was there. After I moved on from KVC, Mercy Vineyard became something of a reconfiguration of KVC and a safe place to land for many. KVC no longer exists but does function as a tiny church group under a different name.

The extent of my role and involvement in turning these places around, or indeed, in failing to turn them around, was relative. In the case of Barneys, I had a particular role on the team that functioned under Peter Holgate's gracious and able lead. In the case of KVC, it was the steepest learning curve of turnaround change. At that point I had not yet added the theory of leading for turnaround change that was taught at Fuller Seminary in my doctoral studies. I still functioned largely on gut feel and what I thought the Spirit was saying and doing. I was also less collaborative and consultative than I am now. I have never been the kind of leader who makes unilateral decisions, but I have become far more intentionally collaborative than before. There are many things that could have been done differently, but I suspect it would not have made any difference. In the practice of turnaround change, there comes a time when a place is too far gone and it needs to shut shop and reconfigure. KVC was an example of such a place. As someone said upon my leaving, "Melt, your presence here was like a plaster stuck over a festering wound. After you left the plaster was ripped off and the wound was still septic." Some people blamed me for leaving the church when we were on an upward trajectory, and I accept whatever apportionment of that blame is mine. However, if the church was dependent on my or anyone else's presence in order to be a flourishing community, it was clearly built on the wrong foundation. I tried to point to the One we worship always, but it seems that in this instance it was not successful.

> *Or to put it another way, you are God's house. Using the gift God gave me as a good architect, I designed blueprints; Apollos is putting up the walls. Let each carpenter who comes on the job take care to build on the foundation! Remember, there is only one foundation, the one already laid: Jesus Christ. Take particular care in picking out your building materials. Eventually there is going to be an inspection. If you use cheap or inferior materials, you'll be found out. The inspection will be thorough and rigorous. You won't get by with a thing. If your work passes inspection, fine; if it doesn't, your part of the building will be torn out and started over.*

But you won't be torn out; you'll survive—but just barely. (1 Cor 3:9-15, MSG)

In the case of ESSA, my role was very relative. ESSA was under accreditation review and needed to show they had a principal if they were to regain accreditation. I came along at just the right time, but God was up to bigger things for them and clearly in my own life too. The call to fixing broken or partially broken things was fully underway by the time I accepted the ESSA contract, and the reality of this being, in part, my call had fully settled on me. I was working toward a doctor of ministry degree at Fuller Seminary that included modules such as "Leading for Turnaround Change" and a doctoral project on succession and transition of leadership.

How I was called to ESSA is a *bigger story* in itself. The big and successful work I had always thought would come my way continued to elude me. I kept being steered back to the small and broken. And it was clearly God's steering, because I certainly was not seeking these places out. I was still looking for that four to five hundred strong congregation the Baptist pastor told me was "mine for the picking."

At the time of the call to ESSA, I was looking for sessional teaching opportunities to boost income. When I dropped my resume their way, I received an email from the dean, who said he thought I might be principal material. I was flown from Cape Town to Pietermaritzburg for an interview and the rest, as they say, is history. The contract as principal followed. The problem for my family was that our youngest daughter Emma was in grade eleven and we were Cape Town based. Pietermaritzburg is 1,160 kilometers from Cape Town, and relatively speaking, a backwater that would never have crossed my mind as a location for a career. I certainly could not afford to move my family there on the salary that was on offer.

An agreement was reached for me to work a cycle of six weeks on and one week off for the year of 2016. The seminary paid for five trips that year for me to move between Cape Town and Pietermaritzburg. I was able to stay in Cape Town for longer stints between semesters. It was a hard year for sure, but doable. Prior to 2015, Pietermaritzburg had never crossed my mind nor my path as to work possibilities. Simply put, it was not on my radar in any way, shape or form. Yet it is where I end up in January 2016.

> The big and successful work I had always thought would come my way continued to elude me. I kept being steered back to the small and broken.

After a few weeks in Pietermaritzburg, Sandra Naicker telephoned. Sandra had been in an undergraduate class I lectured in Urban Mission at Cornerstone in 2003 or 2004. We had not stayed in contact, but she had heard that I had been appointed as the principal of ESSA. She came to visit, with her Bible (ominously) under her arm. We had tea together in the office and caught up. Then she said, "well it's good to know what you have been up to and that your family is well. Let me tell you why I am really here." She explained her work-related involvement with Development Associates International (DAI) from 2005. She was distraught by the current leadership structures and practices in South Africa and had been praying about a solution to the problem. DAI USA, the head office, had a general policy of not getting involved politically in National Ministry Centres outside of the USA.

Sandra shared some of the challenges she was facing, which included the presence of DAI in South Africa for twenty years without the organisation existing formally. It was not registered as an NPO, had no Board of Directors, and was not registered for charitable status, so as a result, could not raise funds locally. No one working for the organisation was able to be registered as a salary earner who legitimately paid taxes to the South African Receiver of Revenue (SARS). There was a bank account in the name of the local Ministry Centre Director (MCD) to receive funds from the USA office. This account was managed by the local MCD and he had seconded a friend to give them access to the account so that he could be held accountable for the way the finances were handled. At that point DAI SA was completely funded by the USA. The MCD had set up an office with a PA, landline, conference room, parking and all amenities charged to DAI USA, from which he ran three private businesses, one property rental, one construction and one consulting business. The MCD was an attorney who told me a few years later that strictly speaking there was nothing illegal or unethical about what he was doing since it was indicative of working smart rather than working hard. Concurrent legal speak then followed when he was challenged.

I listened to Sandra's story and commiserated with her as she shared these challenges. Then, she said that as she was praying for a solution, my name had dropped into her mind. At the time my name came to her, I was still in Cape Town, completely unaware of the existence of ESSA. She thought my name might be her own idea, so she said to the Lord in prayer, "Ok Lord, if that was you, then you need to make him come to Pietermaritzburg." If you are familiar with South Africa, you will understand how crazy the notion of me ending up in Pietermaritzburg was. It was equitable to someone praying in Brandon, Manitoba that a person would be brought there from downtown Vancouver.

Next she asked if I would be open to her praying for me. I answered in the affirmative. She read this Scripture:

> *The Lord Almighty has revealed this in my hearing: "Till your dying day this sin will not be atoned for," says the Lord, the Lord Almighty.*
>
> *This is what the Lord, the Lord Almighty, says:*
>
> *"Go, say to this steward, to Shebna the palace administrator: What are you doing here and who gave you permission to cut out a grave for yourself here, hewing your grave on the height and chiseling your resting place in the rock?*
>
> *"Beware, the Lord is about to take firm hold of you and hurl you away, you mighty man. He will roll you up tightly like a ball and throw you into a large country. There you will die and there the chariots you were so proud of will become a disgrace to your master's house. I will depose you from your office, and you will be ousted from your position.*
>
> *"In that day I will summon my servant, Eliakim son of Hilkiah. I will clothe him with your robe and fasten your sash around him and hand your authority over to him. He will be a father to those who live in Jerusalem and to the people of Judah. I will place on his shoulder the key to the house of David; what he opens no one can shut, and what he shuts no one can open. I will drive him like a peg into a firm place; he will become a seat of honor for the house of his father. All the glory of his family will hang on him: its offspring and offshoots—all its lesser vessels, from the bowls to all the jars.*

> *"In that day," declares the Lord Almighty, "the peg driven into the firm place will give way; it will be sheared off and will fall, and the load hanging on it will be cut down." The Lord has spoken. (Isa 22:14-25, NIV)*

Sandra then prayed and likened me to Eliakim son of Hilkiah. It must have been affirming to me, because I wrote the date of her prophesy next to the Scripture in my Bible. But I also remember it as quite overwhelming. I told her that I had only just come to ESSA and had a job to do. In addition, no one was offering me the MCD position at DAI just yet.

> But God had got my attention through Sandra's visit and prophesy. Most notably, through the answer to her prayer that now saw me, against all odds, in Pietermaritzburg!

I focussed on the task at hand with ESSA and did not have much communication with Sandra until I received a call from her in May inviting me to a DAI conference in Cairo, Egypt. At the time ESSA was in conversation with DAI regarding possibilities around us offering their M.A. in Organizational Leadership as the hosting and accrediting organization in Southern Africa. The invitation to the conference came under this pretext. At the conference I met the international DAI leaders and many spoke of their desires for the organisation in South Africa. It became apparent at the conference that the current MCD was looking for a successor, as he was seventy years old and wanting to retire. The potential successor (not me) was also on the trip to Egypt. On our return from the trip, it was clear that the potential successor was not interested in working for DAI in SA. Through a listening process lasting several months, the Director of DAI east and southern Africa, Nicolas Wafula, unexpectedly offered me the position. The ESSA contract was concluded in December of 2016, and I started as MCD DAI SA in January 2017.

The work at DAI SA was the work of turnaround. By that point, this was my accustomed and usual call. We were to continue our leadership training workshops for the church. In addition, we were to establish the organisation as a legitimate and registered entity, put a Board of Directors and accountability structures in place, open a corporate and tax compliant bank account, and start an effort toward fundraising locally. The policy of DAI at the time was moving toward local Ministry Centres being largely responsible for their own fundraising. Without going into the tedious detail of the processes and challenges along the way, we managed to:

1. Raise over R350,000 locally, which from an unregistered organisation was incredible.
2. Run leadership training workshops with students from the University of the Western Cape and with the AOG in Katlehong (see page 69).
3. Establish a multi-gender and multi-ethnic Board of Directors.
4. Move toward registration as an NPO and charitable fundraising organisation.

Sandra got the organisation registered as an NPO with charitable status and opened a corporate and tax compliant bank account for DAI after my departure for Canada in November 2018. The task we had begun together, she saw through to completion. None of the work done by the team at that time was the kind that people shout from the rooftops, since it is work that should have been done twenty years prior. There was significant embarrassment around the fact that it took two decades to complete these necessary tasks. But they eventually got done. Development Associates South Africa (DASA), as it is now called, continues to thrive and function across southern Africa as an organisation that offers leadership training for the local church.

On accepting the contract to ESSA, I had no idea that it would lead to significant turnaround for two organisations in a three-year period. ESSA regained their B.Th. accreditation and DASA is a legitimate NPO doing significant work across southern Africa.

> No blazing lights, little fanfare, little recognition or appreciation even, but in every way bigger and more important things for the sake of the Kingdom. Things that are foundational to our integrity and witness to a watching and waiting world.

By now, en route to Canada and Yellowknife Vineyard Church, I understood that turnaround work would for sure form at least some part of the next chapter God had called us to.

CHAPTER 17

CONTEMPLATION FOR THE REST OF US

"What we plant in the soil of contemplation we shall reap in the harvest of action."

MEISTER ECKHART

I came to faith in 1990, at a time of renewed interest in the spiritual disciplines and the ancient paths and practices that have served Jesus' people through the ages. Richard Foster wrote his groundbreaking book *Celebration of Discipline* in 1978, which went a long way to bringing the spiritual disciplines back into mainstream Protestantism.[117] Dallas Willard's *Spirit of the Disciplines* was written a decade later and seemed to complete what Foster had begun.[118] The Roman Catholic tradition had of course never veered away from the spiritual disciplines or from contemplation as a way of life. Thomas Merton and others had preceded Foster and Willard by several decades and more than likely influenced them. But it was largely Foster and Willard who made these things accessible again to Protestants and even evangelicals. I am grateful to have come into the faith when I did. I am also glad to have found myself in streams that did not dismiss the broader set of spiritual disciplines aside from prayer and Bible reading.

My rebirth was a rather radical one and was marked by a few things. Most notably, I developed an incredible affection for people I would not have associated with a few months prior. I also had a sudden and voracious appetite for reading. I must have read an average of forty to fifty books a year between 1990 and 2000, and that was before doing any formal Christian studies. Not everything I read was equally helpful! R. J. Rushdoony's *Institutes of Biblical Law* and his thoughts on Christian reconstruction were an early influence that I am thankful to have escaped.[119] In hindsight, it was helpful to have read some of his work since it has had a profound impact on American religious conservatism.

My season of reading on the spiritual disciplines, the contemplative tradition, and the mystics began in the early 1990s. I read Foster and Willard as well as Thomas a Kempis' *The Imitation of Christ*, which I found rather legalistic. These authors inspired me to integrate contemplative spiritual practices into my life and whet my appetite for reading more on the mystics. I read Merton, Brother Lawrence, Teresa of Avilla, St. John of the Cross, Julian of Norwich, Meister Eckhard, Ignatius of Loyola, Hildegard of Bingen, St. Francis of Assisi—you name them, and I read them! I confess that the deeply mystical writings of people like Teresa of Avilla and Hildegard of Bingen never quite cut it for me. They were far too removed from life and reality.

> I am, at best, a busy and pioneering practical mystic and a tamed rebel. I need my spiritual disciplines and practices to be anchored into real life. Because, after all, as those philosophers Opus sing, "life is life."

Ignatius Loyola, as a former soldier, was used to being always on the move. His spiritual practices worked better for me. Ignatian spirituality seemed to me to be more anchored to life. *I was not looking for an escape.* But I was seeking disciplines and practices that would keep me firmly in the vine (John 15).

Being called into the Anglican Church in 2001, which is significantly influenced by the Benedictine tradition, assisted me in the journey toward integrating the spiritual disciplines and contemplative practices as part and parcel of faith and life. I grew to value the liturgical calendar and the rhythms of the Church year—Advent, Christmas, Lent, Easter, Ordinary Time—using the *Anglican Book of Common Praye*r *(BCP)* and more. The practice of morning prayer and evening prayer from the *(BCP)*, with the added Benedictine practice of "looking up" at midday, settled on me. Although as a morning person my evening efforts were, and still are, rather wasted.

> Whilst I grew to appreciate these ancient paths and practices, I never grew to value them to the extent that I was willing to serve them. I felt that all these things only ever serve us. It was Jesus who said, *"the Sabbath was made for man, not man for the Sabbath" (Mk 2:27, NIV)*.

On coming into the Anglican Church and being introduced to the liturgy and other practices, two incidents revealed that I would struggle to be a good Anglican long-term. First, I was asked to put together an order of service for a special event. I set aside a block of twenty minutes for worship in music. The music interfered with the programme that the rector had in mind. I was instructed to cut the music to ten minutes max. I then asked whether we could not rather "muck about with the liturgy" to allow a decent slot for the worship in music, which was more important to me. I was told in no uncertain terms that one did not "muck about with the liturgy." Second, one day at Barneys the archdeacon came to do his quarterly rounds and I was the only cleric (deacon) available to show him around. In the largely liberal Diocese of Table Bay, the staff of the Anglican cathedral in the city of Cape Town referred to Barneys as the "evangelicals on the hill" since we were a few kilometers uphill toward Table Mountain. It was from the cathedral that the archdeacon came to us. On his inspection rounds he asked me to unlock the aumbry, which is a cupboard where the ***reserved sacrament*** was kept.

> The ***reserved sacrament*** is bread and wine consecrated by a priest that is set aside after Communion and stored in a tabernacle for later use. It is typically used for the sick or for those who cannot attend the Eucharist service. The reserved sacrament is usually kept in a locked container, often called a tabernacle or aumbry, placed on or near the altar, and is a visible symbol of Christ's presence.

When I unlocked the aumbry, there were three Shure mics stored in the cupboard along with the reserved sacrament. I was asked by the

Archdeacon what these "musical instruments" were doing there. It was not the right time to mention that I had significant theological reservations around the concept of a reserved sacrament in the first place, so I just made a sarcastic comment (an acknowledged weakness of mine). I said, "well Andrew, you know we are evangelical, so for us music is a sacrament." He said, "and I suppose you think that is funny"—which of course, I did.

But in all this, I would like to propose that we do not throw any babies out with any bath water due to nuances in belief or expression. There are things in the historical mainstream churches that the charismatic tradition honestly can embrace and learn from. My fondness for the Anglican Church and traditions remains firmly intact. The spiritual disciplines, an intentionally more contemplative posture, and what John Mark Comer calls the "ruthless elimination of hurry"[120] are all tried and tested ancient spiritual practices that have anchored the Church for 2,000 years. In the Pentecostal and charismatic traditions, these things have often been eschewed. I have never really understood why they would be rejected. The mystics are, after all, much about the experiential and are in many ways the ancient equivalent of the modern charismatic tradition.

Coming into the Vineyard in 2006 was yet another move toward making me a semi-contemplative, or so I call myself. I am contemplative and have found the practices and disciplines that work for me—more about that shortly. Like Foster says in the opening to *Celebration of Discipline*, every time I come to the disciplines, I come as a returning novice. I need more of these simple yet bigger things. One of my first Vineyard pastoral retreats in South Africa involved Alexander Venter[121] leading us all in a contemplative exercise with a little flickering candle we were to focus on. I recall Alexander saying something along the lines of "inside each one of us there is a hidden Roman Catholic." At the time I remember thinking, "that's probably why I still feel guilty about so much." But more seriously, this to illustrate that the contemplative stream is a part of Vineyard, although it has, in my thinking, been under-emphasised. Both David and Anita Ruis, who have led AVC Canada for the past decade, are deeply contemplative people and this characteristic has shaped Vineyard Canada for the good.

> The founder of Vineyard, John Wimber, was initially ordained as a Quaker minister. Quakers are deeply contemplative and are also pacifist. Those roots influenced Vineyard churches, some more than others. I often feel like we have over-emphasised parts of our heritage and rather radically under-emphasised others.

An article in *Patheos* from September of 2019 says that John Wimber was mostly known as the leader of the third wave charismatic movement before he died in 1997.[122] The article states that Wimber embraced signs and wonders and spiritual gifts, but that he is not particularly remembered as a biblical pacifist. *But a pacifist he was*, even though he did not preach on the topic significantly. In later years, Wimber described pacifism as a theological value he had embraced during his years with the Society of Friends, the Quaker church. He explained that when he was personally attacked, his first response was to turn the other cheek.

Wimber's pacifism evolved over the years. In 1992 he clarified that non-violence should not be confused with personal passivity.[123] The Gospel, he said, must be defended. Wimber's path reflected the trajectory of many American Anabaptists who have moved from a position of non-resistance to a position of active peacemaking. Evil should be resisted, they say, but not violently. Pacifism has never been a popular doctrine in practice. Wimber was operating in a particularly fraught time, not dissimilar from our own. Parts of the third wave charismatic movement were already veering towards Christian dominionism and seven mountain theology, in which Christians are mandated to occupy or invade key sectors of society, education, religion, family, business, government, military, arts, entertainment and the media. Rushdoony's influence had begun to manifest.

Wimber's Quakerism didn't die with him. Absolutely not. The charismatic practices and methods of listening prayer, waiting, and gender egalitarianism of the Vineyard have deep roots in Wimber's Quakerism. So too the influence is seen in our dial-down posture in worship and our general acceptance of waiting and not fearing silence. We tend to trust that the Spirit is doing what the Spirit does, so we do not presume to tell him what he ought to be doing. Unfortunately, from my perspective, pacifism did not get embedded in the Vineyard movement's DNA to the extent that some of the more contemplative postures clearly did, even where they are not named as such.

Let's return to the contemplative posture and the spiritual disciplines then. Some of the ancient paths under consideration are things that we can and ought to embrace communally, such as confession. *We are a confessing people.* Not just in the sense of us confessing sin to someone—which is a good spiritual practice to be sure. We are a confessional faith. We confess (proclaim) the Lordship of Christ, and we confess our faith anytime we read the creeds together. We confess our faith when there is *kerygma* (proclamation) of any kind. These are all practices that keep us communally anchored into the vine. One year ago at Yellowknife

Vineyard Church, we had an evening Tenebrae service on the Thursday night before Good Friday. *It is a service of darkness or shadows.* A man in his seventies who was a relatively new believer wrote to tell me it was spiritually the most significant thing he had ever attended. It was a tiny evening service attended by perhaps twenty or twenty-five people. People tend not to come to evening events in a place where temperatures drop to -20 degrees even around Easter.

> But a bigger thing was happening than my paltry metrics. Someone was being deeply and profoundly touched by the Spirit of Jesus through a service that has its origins in the monastic communities of medieval times.

My naturally supernatural bent and inclination is apostolically (lower case "a") missional. I am a shepherd and a missional type catalyzer in fairly equal proportion. If you ask me to do something, it will get done properly. If it is worth doing, then it is worth doing well. With that kind of hard-wiring, *I desperately need the contemplative* to allow me to rest, recuperate, and lean into Jesus, or I will get to the place where I am running on empty and burn out. It is as simple as that. The spiritual disciplines are for me a corrective gift of God. *I am not naturally a contemplative.* Very few, if any, apostolic types are. It is my conviction that it is usually the people who reject the ancient spiritual paths and practices who significantly need them.

Individually, there are many inward and outward spiritual disciplines we can practice to lean closer into Jesus. As a semi-contemplative, I do not feel qualified to write in depth on any one of these. Willard and Foster remain wonderful starting points for learning more about spiritual disciplines. My contemporary "go to" contemplatives are Dan Wilt of Asbury Seminary and Vineyard USA (and formerly Canada) and John Mark Comer. They are two of many. The extent to which I am willing to teach on spiritual disciplines is simply to encourage God's people not to dismiss the ancient paths that have been practiced by the Church through the ages and exist to keep us anchored. I am also happy to share a little about the disciplines that work for me, recognising that each of us is different. Each of us is wired uniquely (1 Cor 12) and we each need to find those things that work for us.

The disciplines that tend to work for me are solitude, silence, prayer, journaling, worship, study, writing, confession, submission and simplicity. It is not that I do not fast, meditate, celebrate, steward, evangelise, sacrifice, practice Sabbath, memorise, or do Lectio or the Examen. I do those things too, from time to time, but they are not a consistent part of my routine. I have a particular rhythm that I know feeds my soul. We all need routine to some extent. We are all "liturgical" people in that sense.

I currently have a group of four men who are linked in a chat group. I freely and often use that space confessionally to hold myself accountable. I am also, as I type this in April of 2025, busy reconnecting myself with a spiritual director, which I have not had in some years.

If the contemplative stream is something you have been taught to distrust or you feel that the spiritual disciplines are pointless, I urge you to reconsider. Practicing the spiritual disciplines is a small thing that helps to keep us grafted into the bigger thing, who is Jesus.

Renewal by God's Spirit never replaces the tried and tested. If the signs of renewal become the thing, they will keep us from the small things that are bigger things in keeping us anchored to the big thing. Renewal only enhances these things since everything is renewed.

CONCLUSION

When setting out to write, I hoped that *Bigger Things* would achieve three goals. I wanted it to be educational, somewhat prophetic, and narrative/biographical. It is mostly written to and for the Vineyard, but of course one hopes for a broader footprint. I am increasingly ecumenical and really value the whole Church. John Wimber used to take heat from some quarters for how much he loved the whole Church in the whole world. I think I am in that place too. Vineyard is the tribe I call home, but I feel free to draw from many other places, recognising that God's people come in all the colours of the rainbow. With such a rich heritage of tradition, it becomes rather anaemic and counter-productive to be fixated only on "my own."

In March of 2025, Larry Levy shared something with me which had been shared with him by a Roman Catholic friend who had heard it at an ecumenical prayer gathering in London, England. This is what was shared: "500 years ago, we were burning one another at the stake. In time to come, perhaps not too distantly in the future, I suspect it might well be that we will be laying down our lives for one another." I believe it. I had my own recent and profound awareness of Jesus on the doorstep of a Roman Catholic Church in Croatia in 2023. But more of that in the next book.

The biographical and narrative parts of *Bigger Things* are meant to support the educational and prophetic bits as real-life practical illustrations of the theology on offer. This flow was born from my frustration that formal theology is often made inaccessible to Jesus' people because it is usually articulated in such an abstract—removed from real life—way. I hope to have stumbled upon a different way of doing theology. It's not a new or unique way, since it's the way many preachers preach, but it is not the way formal theology is usually taught. I hope that the narrative sections of *Bigger Things* make the theology accessible, authentic and intimate. Those are Vineyard's values for worship in music. Doing theology is an act of worship, so there is no reason the values should differ.

If I am to do more of the same moving ahead, I would love to hear how this way of writing was received by you. Please email me at melt.vanderspuy@newjoychurch.com.

In the process of writing *Bigger Things*, I learned that formal studies have enabled me to write quickly. I tend toward being a little too concise. When I am done saying something, I tend to be done, without embellishing or expanding too much. I am hoping this lands me in writing books that are accessible at around 200 pages. I try to write as I speak and will continue in that vein. As I say to my Canadian friends: it's not me who has the accent, it's you.

Grace and peace,
Melt

Soli Deo Gloria

APPENDIX

SMALL THINGS	BIGGER THINGS
The Spirit poured out tongues	The Spirit poured out on the nations
Speaks powerful truths	Speaks truth to power
Bible is the final authority	Holy Spirit is the final authority
Under/over-realised eschatology	Inaugurated eschatology
Bounded/fuzzy set belonging	Centred-set belonging
Disqualified/shamed perpetrators	Reconciled bridge-builders
Gifts are the sign of following Jesus	Suffering is the sign of following Jesus
A successful ministry	A ministry abandoned to Jesus
Redeem spirit—jettison matter	Redeem it all—spirit, body, creation, cosmos
Manifestations are the focal point	The making-new of Jesus is the focal point
Post your big experiences	Ponder your experiences in silence & obscurity
Dominion = power over people	Servanthood = power under people
Pray for justice	Courageously bring justice
Leader sets direction for community	Co-discerning direction in community
The single special prophetic voice	The communal common prophetic voice
Propping up the status quo	Stepping into turnarounds
Serve or dismiss spiritual disciplines	Engage in disciplines to serve bigger things

HOW PROTESTANTS CARRY THE SPIRIT OF GOD

Belief that the gifts of the Spirit are no longer active	Active belief in the gifts of the Holy Spirit
God only speaks to us through His Word	God speaks through His Word and Spirit today
BIBLE ONLY (Non-Charismatics)	SIGNS AND WONDERS (Charismatics)
Dispensational Theology	Baptism of the Spirit

RADICAL MIDDLE

LEADING INTERPRETIVE KEYS AND PRACTICES

Obedience to the written Word of God	Everyone gets to play their part	Seeking the Anointing
NOT YET	ALREADY/NOT YET	ALREADY (Kingdom now)
Under-realized eschatology	Inaugurated eschatology	Over-realized eschatology
Teaching of the Word	People of God	Ministers/Ministries
Paul and Epistles	Gospels	Book of Acts
Written scriptures are the only Prophetic voice	A prophetic people: Ministry gifts are verbs	Anointed Prophets hold offices
Preaching of the Word	Authority—being authorized	Demonstrations of power

RECOMMENDED FURTHER READING

The following selections are resources that have been helpful to me and combine academic rigour with reader accessibility.

ESCHATOLOGY AND THE KINGDOM OF GOD

Derek J. Morphew, *Breakthrough: Discovering the Kingdom* (Cape Town: Vineyard International, 1991).

N. T. Wright, *Surprised by Hope: Rethinking Heaven, the Resurrection and the Mission of the Church* (San Francisco: Harper One, 2014).

Scot McKnight, *Kingdom Conspiracy: Returning to the Radical Mission of the Local Church* (Grand Rapids, MI: Brazos Press, 2018).

Dallas Willard, *The Divine Conspiracy: Rediscovering Our Hidden Life in God* (New York: Harper One, 2005).

BLOGS

davidfitch@substack.com
michaelfbird@substack.com
scotmcknight@substack.com

jemartisby@substack.com
bethfelkerjones@substack.com
www.snowmanconsulting.com

GNOSTICISM AND NEO-PLATONIC THOUGHT

Derek J. Morphew, *The Spiritual Spider Web: A Study of Ancient and Contemporary Gnosticism* (Cape Town: VBI, 2000). Note: This material is available at no cost and a PDF copy can be emailed on request.

David Brakke, *The Gnostics: Myth, Ritual and Diversity in Early Christianity* (Boston: Harvard University Press, 2010).

BIBLICAL INTERPRETATION

Gordon D. Fee & Douglas Stuart, *How to Read the Bible for All Its Worth,* 4th ed. (Grand Rapids, MI: Zondervan, 2014).

ON TRINITY

Recognising that few have the time or inclination to read the great Trinitarian theologians Athanasius of Alexandria, the Cappadocian Fathers, Augustine, Tertullian and, in our times, Karl Bath, the only book I recommend on Trinity is an exceptionally accessible primer that gives a good overview on ancient and modern approaches to Trinity as well as different views on it.

John Fischer, *Towards a Kingdom Theology of the Trinity* (Cape Town: Rory Mole Publishing, 2017). Note: This book is available at no cost and a PDF copy can be emailed on request.

APOCALYPTIC LITERATURE

Scot McKnight, *Revelation for the Rest of Us: A Prophetic Call to Follow Jesus as a Dissident Disciple* (Grand Rapids, MI: Zondervan, 2023).

SPIRITUAL DISCIPLINES

Richard J. Foster, *Celebration of Discipline: The Path to Spiritual Growth* (New York: Harper Collins, 1978).

_______, *Prayer: Finding the Heart's True Home* (London: Hodder & Stoughton, 1992).

Dallas Willard, *The Spirit of the Disciplines: Understanding How God Changes Lives* (New York: Harper Collins, 2009).

John Mark Comer, *Practising the Way: Be with Jesus, Become like Him, Do as He Did* (Multnomah, CO: WaterBrook, 2024).

_______, *The Ruthless Elimination of Hurry: How to Stay Emotionally Healthy and Spiritually Alive in the Chaos of the Modern World* (Multnomah, CO: WaterBrook, 2019).

WEBSITES

Renovaire.org
DanWilt.com

ENDNOTES

1 N. T. Wright and Michael F. Bird, *Jesus and the Powers: Christian Political Witness in an Age of Totalitarian Terror and Dysfunctional Democracies* (Grand Rapids: Zondervan, 2024).

2 For a more thorough discussion on eschatology, see Chapter 4.

3 See 1 Peter 4:1, 5:10; Romans 5:3-4, 8:18; Matthew 10:38; 2 Corinthians 1:5; Philippians 3:10; Acts 9:16; and John 13:8, among others.

4 I am using Michael Bird's term "building *for* the kingdom" throughout in preference to "building *the* kingdom" because it guards against overtly triumphalist claims.

5 St. John's Parish Wynberg is a group of six churches within the greater Anglican Diocese of Table Bay who identify as Anglican, Evangelical and Charismatic.

6 The New Wine movement in the UK has seen significant cooperation between Anglican and Vineyard churches that carried over to an extent into South Africa.

7 For a more detailed discussion on using the prophetic gifting responsibly, see Chapter 15.

8 Walter Thiessen, *Glimpses of a Good Life: Rhythms and Practices that Invite Wholeness* (New Brunswick: St. Stephens Publishing, 2013).

9 Richard Foster, as quoted by Ted Harro in Renovare blog on March 7, 2025.

10 See 1 Corinthians 14. I happen to pray in tongues and am incredibly grateful for the gift. However, I am unwilling to make more of the gift than Scripture makes of it.

11 Stanley Hauerwas and Will Willemon, *Resident Aliens: Life in the Christian Colony* (Nashville: Abingdon Press, 1990), 3.

12 Beth M. Stovell, "Moving from 'Them' to 'Us': A Biblical Theology for Diaspora Ministry," in *Beyond Hospitality: Migration, Multiculturalism and the Church,* eds. Charles Cook, Lauren Goldbeck, and Lora Joy Tira-Dimangondayao (Toronto, Canada: Tyndale Academic Press, 2020), 3.

13 Ibid., 1.

14 Michael Bird, blog, February 2025.

15 https://www.un.org

16 Karl Meuller, "The Mission of the Church among the Canadian Diaspora: Developing New Canadian Leaders for the Church in Canada," resource for DAI Canada (Development Associates International, 2019), 1.

17 Chris Chilvers, *Church Times*, 5 September 2007.

18 Douglas Stuart and Gordon D. Fee, *How to Read the Bible for All Its Worth: A Guide to Understanding the Bible* (Grand Rapids: Zondervan, 2014).

19 See the book by the same name. Bill Jackson, *The Quest for the Radical Middle: A History of the Vineyard* (Cape Town: Vineyard International, 2006).

20 Melt van der Spuy, , "Continuous Sustainable Succession Planning: A Guide to Identify and Train Leaders for AVC Canada," Fuller Theological Seminary, 2021.

21 David Ruis, "When the Church Seeks First the Kingdom," Vineyard Canada National Gathering podcast, 7 August 2018, https://www.vineyard.ca/index.php?topic=410.0.

22 Supernatural is probably a poor word to use relating to signs and wonders. We are dealing with the God who is supernatural in every way. I use the word nonetheless because it might promote a clearer understanding of what is under discussion.

23 Rob Bell, *What is the Bible: How an Ancient Library of Poems, Letters and Stories can Transform the Way You Think and Feel about Everything* (New York: Harper One, 2017).

24 van der Spuy, "Continuous Sustainable Succession Planning".

25 Beth Stovell (Ph.D. McMaster Divinity College) is currently Associate Professor of Old Testament at Ambrose Seminary of Ambrose University in Calgary, Alberta, Canada. Previously, Beth taught at St. Thomas University in Miami Gardens, Florida and as an instructor and guest lecturer at McMaster Divinity College, Regent College, and Pacific Life Bible College. Beth is a colleague and long-standing member of Epic Vineyard Church in Calgary and serves on AVC Canada's National Leadership Team.

26 This content is partially derived from a Ridley College Chapel message by Michael F. Bird from 2024.

27 The primary task of the Holy Spirit in all things, always, is to reveal and bring glory to Jesus, the Son.

28 Chapter 9 offers some insight into Gnosticism and neo-Platonic thought and its infiltration into the twenty-first century Church.

29 See Rabbi David Frankel, "Who did What to Whom in the Tent," SBL e-journal (2017).

30 Leonard Sweet, *So Beautiful: Divine Design for Life and the Church* (Colorado Springs, CO: Cook, 2009), 23.

31 Wright and Bird, *Jesus and the Powers*, 36.

32 *John Wimber's Pastoral Letters*, compiled by Derek Morphew (Vineyard International, 2020), 142-143.

33 I provide a rough breathing accent on the Greek ὁμοουσιος since this is one accent or diacritic that is useful to represent the Greek form of the word, as it indicates rough breathing. In every other instance of Greek, I have shown the word without any accentuation for consistency.

34 For further reading on Trinitarian formulation, please see the addendum to *Bigger Things.*

35 A phrase likely coined by Brevard Childs.

36 Todd Rutkowski, *Our Beautiful Mess* (Lodestar Consulting, 2025).

37 Richard B. Hayes, *Reading Backwards: Figural Christology and the Fourfold Gospel Witness* (Waco, TX: Baylor University Press, 2014).

38 Ibid., 86.

39 N.T. Wright, *The Day the Revolution Began: Reconsidering the Meaning of Jesus's Crucifixion* (San Francisco: Harper One, 2018). This book makes frequent reference to 1 Corinthians 15:3-4 and emphasises that Jesus' death and resurrection are in accordance with the Scriptures and fulfill the hopes of the Old Testament.

40 N.T. Wright, *On Earth as in Heaven: Daily Wisdom for Twenty-First Century Christians* (San Francisco: Harper One, 2022).

41 See for example Matthew 12:32; 2 Peter 3:3; Mark 10:30; Luke 18:30, 20:34-36; Ephesians 2:7; 1 Timothy 6:19; 1 Corinthians 2:68; and Isaiah 41:23, 65:17.

42 *The Hobbit*, directed by Peter Jackson (2012).

43 Derek J. Morphew, *Breakthrough: Discovering the Kingdom* (Cape Town: Vineyard International, 2007).

44 See the book by the same name. G.E. Ladd, *The Presence of the Future* (Grand Rapids, MI: W. B. Eerdmans, 1996).

45 More expanded thought on suffering in Chapter 7.

46 See Revelation 2:1-7, 2 Timothy 3:11, and 1 Peter 2:19.

47 Wright and Bird, *Jesus and the Powers*, 36.

48 Paul Hiebert, *The Gospel in Human Contexts: Anthropological Explorations for Contemporary Missions* (Grand Rapids, MI: Baker Academic, 2009).

49 Figure taken from *Centered-Set Church: Community and Discipleship Without Judgmentalism* by Mark D. Baker, copyright © 2021 by Mark D. Baker. Used by permission of InterVarsity Press, www.ivpress.com.

50 https://www.britannica.com/topic/Group-Areas-Act-of-1950-South-Africa

51 The South African Border War, also known as the Namibian War of Independence, and sometimes denoted in South Africa as the Angolan Bush War, was a largely asymmetric conflict that occurred in Namibia (then South West Africa), Zambia, and Angola from 26 August 1966 to 21 March 1990. It was fought between the South African Defense Force (SADF) and the People's Liberation Army of Namibia (PLAN), an armed wing of the South West African People's Organisation (SWAPO). The South African Border War was closely intertwined with the Angolan Civil War.

52 Operation Protea was a military operation during the South African Border War and Angolan Civil War in which the SADF destroyed several SWAPO bases in Angola. It took place from 23 August to 4 September 1981. Up to 5,000 SADF soldiers occupied the Cunene province of Angola. *This is offered just in case you were looking for me on those dates and wondering where I was.*

53 The South West Africa People's Organisation, now the ruling party of independent Namibia.

54 Os Guinness, *The Call: Finding and Fulfilling the Central Purpose of Your Life* (Nashville, TN: Thomas Nelson, 2018).

55 Betty's Bay is a small holiday town situated on the Overberg coast of South Africa's Western Cape Province. It is located 100 kilometers from Cape Town beneath the Kogelberg Mountains.
56 Caleb currently pastors Bristol Vineyard in the UK and is the son of David Pederson, the National Director of Vineyard in South Africa.
57 Dietrich Bonhoeffer, *The Cost of Discipleship*, reprint (New York: Macmillan, 1995).
58 van der Spuy, *Continuous Sustainable Succession Planning*, 125.
59 Derek Morphew, *The Spiritual Spider Web: A Study in Ancient and Contemporary Gnosticism* (Cape Town: Vineyard International, 2000).
60 David Brakke, *The Gnostics: Myth, Ritual and Diversity in Early Christianity* (Boston: Harvard University Press, 2012).
61 Morphew, *The Spiritual Spider Web*, 12.
62 Unless we are of the school that rejects experience completely, even though the Bible is brimming with it.
63 Chapter 17 offers additional parameters in this regard.
64 Sweet, *So Beautiful*, 25.
65 Wright and Bird, *Jesus and the Powers*, 26.
66 http://news.bbc.co.uk/2/hi/uk_news/politics/7136682.stm
67 Rodney Stark, *The Rise of Christianity: How the Obscure, Marginal Jesus Movement Became the Dominant Religious Force in the Western World in a Few Centuries* (San Francisco: Harper One, 1997).
68 Sectarians bypass Scriptures such as Matthew 5:13-16 that call us to be salt and light in this world for the sake of the Kingdom. Hints of this kind of thinking are seen in the conspiratorial thinking that sees the World Council of Churches and the ecumenical movement as utterly corrupt and evil. Its outworking is often evident in doomsday and end time obsessions. "Jesus is coming to snatch us away from this dreadfully wicked place" rather than us as ambassadors for Jesus

redeeming this good but fallen world with him in anticipation of him making all things new.

69 "You Make Beautiful Things," track #2 on Michael Gungor, *Beautiful Things*, 2010.

70 For a more detailed consideration of contemporary prophesy, see Chapter 15.

71 Eugene H. Peterson, *A Long Obedience in the Same Direction: Discipleship in an Instant Society* (Downers Grove, IL: IVP Books, 2000).

72 Eddie Gibbs and Ian Coffey, *Church Next: Quantum Changes in Christian Ministry* (Downers Grove, IL: InterVarsity Press, 2001).

73 J. J. Kritzinger, P. G. J. Meiring, and W. A. Saayman, *On Being Witnesses* (Cottonwood, CA: Orion, 1994), 40.

74 *John Wimber's Pastoral Letters*, 111.

75 Kritzinger, Meiring, and Saayman, *On Being Witnesses*, 41.

76 *John Wimber's Pastoral Letters*, 87.

77 Ibid.

78 Ibid., 94-98.

79 Asbury University saw a spontaneous, student-led prayer and worship event starting on 8 February 2023 and lasting for over two weeks.

80 Peterson, *A Long Obedience in the Same Direction.*

81 Michael Green, *I Believe in the Holy Spirit: Biblical Teaching for the Church Today* (Grand Rapids, MI: W. B. Eerdmans, 1975), 68.

82 William Revel Moody, *The Life of D. L. Moody: By His Son* (Greensboro, MD: Delmarva, 1900), 146-147.

83 Thomas Jay Oord, *The Death of Omnipotence and Birth of Amipotence* (Grasmere, ID: SacraSage Press, 2023).

84 David Fitch, blog, January 2025.

85 Ibid.

86 *John Wimber's Pastoral Letters*, 25.

87 Shane Claiborne, RNS blog, January 2025.

88 Frederick Douglass, *Narrative of the Life of Frederick Douglass, an American* Slave, ed. Deborah E. McDowell (Oxford Paperbacks, 2009).

89 William L. Shire, *The Rise and Fall of the Third Reich: A History of Nazi Germany* (Blackstone Audio, 1960).

90 Scot McKnight, blog, 1 February 2025.

91 Attributed to John Wesley, source unknown.

92 Fitch, blog, 2025.

93 Rutkowski, *Our Beautiful Mess.*

94 Lamott, quoted in McKnight, blog, 2025.

95 Ibid.

96 Sauron is the title character and the main antagonist of J. R. R. Tolkien's *The Lord of the Rings*, where he rules the land of Mordor. He aims to rule the whole of Middle-earth using the power of the One Ring, which he has lost and seeks to recapture. In the same work, he is identified as the necromancer of Tolkien's earlier novel *The Hobbit.*

97 The character Bozo the Clown was created by Alan Livingstone for a series of children's books.

98 Lord Voldemort is a fictional character and the main antagonist in the *Harry Potter* series of novels by J. K. Rowling.

99 The Shire is a fictional region in J.R.R. Tolkien's Middle-earth, primarily known as the home of the hobbits. It's a peaceful, rural area in the region of Eriador, described as a beautiful, fertile land where hobbits thrive. The Shire is a Free Land, protected by the Reunited Kingdom, and largely shielded from the rest of Middle-earth's conflicts.

100 Middle-earth is the fictional continent that serves as the primary setting for many of J.R.R. Tolkien's fantasy works, including *The*

Hobbit, *The Lord of the Rings*, and *The Silmarillion*. It is a vast land populated by elves, dwarves, hobbits, orcs, and men, among other species, and features a rich history and mythology.

101 Dan Wilt, blog, March 2025. Dan is an Asbury Theological Seminary professor, author, teacher and songwriter who has pastored Vineyard churches in Canada and in the USA.

102 This chapter draws considerably from private conversations and correspondences between David Ruis and the author.

103 Stanley Hauerwas, quoted in *Christianity Today*, March 2025.

104 Walter Brueggemann, *Reality, Grief and Hope: Three Urgent Prophetic Tasks* (Grand Rapids, MI: W. B. Eerdmans, 2014).

105 Willie James Jennings, *Acts: A Theological Commentary on the Bible* (Louisville, KY: Westminster John Knox Press, 2017), 124.

106 Ibid., 133.

107 Tom Wright, podcast, October 2023, https://katebowler.com/podcasts/the-mystery-of-god/.

108 Dale B. Martin, *The Corinthian Body* (London: Yale University Press, 1995).

109 Charles L. Campbell, *1 Corinthians: A Theological Commentary on the Bible* (Louisville, KY: Westminster John Knox Press, 2018), 231-232.

110 Ibid.

111 "Bread for the Hungry," in *The Metropolitan Tabernacle Pulpit Sermons* vol. 7 (London: Passmore & Alabaster, 1861), 565.

112 Tom Wright, *Paul for Everyone: 2 Corinthians* (Society for Promoting Christian Knowledge, 2004), 131-132.

113 Amos Yong, *Revelation: A Theological Commentary on the Bible* (Louisville, KY: Westminster John Knox Press, 2021), 78.

114 Ibid., 81-82.

115 *The Book of Common Prayer and the Administration of the Sacraments* (Anglican Liturgy Press, 2019), 146.

116 https://ikhayalethemba.org.za/

117 Richard J. Foster, *Celebration of Discipline: The Path to Spiritual Growth* (New York: Harper Collins, 1978).

118 Dallas Willard, *The Spirit of the Disciplines: Understanding How God Changes Lives* (New York: Harper Collins, 2009).

119 Rousas John Rushdoony, *The Institutes of Biblical Law* (Vallecito, CA: Ross House Books, 2020). Rushdoony was a radical influence on American conservatism.

120 John Mark Comer, *The Ruthless Elimination of Hurry: How to Stay Emotionally Healthy and Spiritually Alive in the Chaos of the Modern World* (New York: WaterBrook, 2019).

121 Alexander Venter is a well-known Vineyard theologian, pastor and author. He has written, amongst other things, *Doing Church, Doing Healing* and *Doing Reconcilliation*. Alexander is a former colleague from Vineyard South Africa.

122 Patheos blog, “Unexpected Sites of Christian Pacifism: John Wimber edition,” 25 September 2019.

123 John Wimber, Vineyard Position Paper #1, “Why I Respond to Criticism,” May 1992.

ABOUT THE AUTHOR

Melt van der Spuy is a pastor, seminary professor, mentor and sometime NPO leader. After fifteen years of management in logistics and distribution, he stepped into a first church call and the world of Christian leadership in 2001. Melt is a South African who has lived and worked in the NWT and BC provinces of Canada since 2018.

Ordained Anglican, he started attending a Vineyard church in 2006. Melt has pastored two Vineyard churches in SA and two in Canada. He holds an M.Th. in Systematics, Missions, and Homiletics from Stellenbosch University in South Africa and a Doctorate in Ministry from Fuller Seminary in Leadership and Succession Studies.

Melt and his wife Anida have three biological daughters, an adopted son and daughter, and a three-year-old grandson. Their children, sons-in-law and grandson all reside in South Africa, apart from their youngest daughter who lives in the Netherlands.

Melt and Anida live with one foot in Canada and one in South Africa. In addition to pastoring, Melt serves on the National Leadership Team of Vineyard Canada and on various Vineyard task teams and committees, with a felt call to mediation, transition, succession and leading for turnaround change. He is a part time affiliate professor of mentoring at Kairos University in Sioux Falls, USA. Although published academically, *Bigger Things* is his first published book.

In a former life Melt was a first-class rugby player in South Africa and is an avid rugby supporter. Since relocating to BC, he is back on the golf course and tries to play every week. Melt and Anida—who is a chef—are avid foodies who love Jesus, family, wine, sports, and travel.

www.ingramcontent.com/pod-product-compliance
Lightning Source LLC
LaVergne TN
LVHW050618100826
845148LV00011B/1640

9798385270415